# Forgiveness After Infidelity

A Step-by-Step Guide to Heal Your Heart and
Rebuild Your Marriage After Infidelity

## Jeffrey D. Murrah

Restore The Family Press

# Contents

# From Betrayal to Healing

"Forgiveness isn't my best thing. Easier staying pissed. But I'm tired of being pissed all the time. Tired of feeling hurt by stuff than can never be fixed because it is an indelible part of the past."
- Ellen Hopkins

When the person you love and trust most in the world betrays you, it shatters the very foundation of your reality. The person you thought you could count on isn't as dependable as you thought. The pain of infidelity can feel unbearable, like a searing knife straight through the heart. If you're reading this book, you probably know this pain all too well. Maybe you discovered incriminating texts on your spouse's phone, uncovered secrets and lies that had been hidden for months or years or heard the devastating confession you never saw coming.

Take the story of Lena and Eric. Their journey through betrayal began on what started as an ordinary Tuesday evening. Lena arrived home from work to find Eric sitting at the kitchen table, his face etched with guilt and anguish. "Lena, there's something I need to tell you," he began, his voice shaking. The next few words out of his mouth decimated life as she knew it: "I've been having an affair."

At that moment, Lena's world crumbled. She felt like she couldn't breathe like the walls were closing in around her. How could this be happening? Not them, not after 15 years of marriage and two beautiful children. Surely, it had to be some awful misunderstanding or a cruel joke. But the harsh reality set in as Eric poured out the sordid details of his months-long fling with a coworker. This was no joke. This was her new world - one filled with excruciating pain, suffocating anger, and unrelenting questions.

If you're in the midst of the storm of infidelity right now, know that you're not alone. So many have sat where you're sitting, crumpled on the bathroom floor, crying tears they didn't know they had. They've lain awake for nights on end, replaying every moment of their marriage, searching for the signs they missed. And they've raged at the unfairness of it all, the magnitude of the betrayal, and the audacity of the lies.

But there is hope. Just as Lena found her way to the other side, so can you. It won't be a quick or easy journey, and there will be times you doubt you'll make it through. But with time, support, and a lot of hard work, you can begin to heal. You can learn how to work through and talk about your emotions, set boundaries, and care for yourself. Most importantly, you can discover the power of forgiveness - not just for your spouse, but for yourself.

Forgiveness is the key that unlocks the prison of bitterness and pain. It lets you release the anger and hurt that eats you alive and find peace amidst the chaos. Please hear this: forgiveness is not about letting your spouse off the hook or condoning their actions. It's not about "forgetting" or magically returning to how things were before. Rather, forgiveness is about freeing yourself. It's about reclaiming your life and refusing to let the betrayal define you. It's about healing your heart so you can move forward, whether that's with your spouse or on your own.

In the pages of this book, we'll walk through the forgiveness process that has transformed countless lives and helped so many find hope and healing after infidelity. We'll debunk common myths about forgiveness, explore the incredible benefits, and identify the barriers that keep us stuck. The book will guide you step-by-step through the journey of letting go, shifting perspectives, and rebuilding trust. We'll chart a path forward, envisioning and creating a life after betrayal that is rich with meaning, joy, and love.

Hold onto hope, no matter how lost, alone, or broken you feel right now. What happened to you is not okay, and it's not your fault. You didn't deserve this pain and don't have to stay stuck in it. Forgiveness is possible, healing is possible, and a brighter future is possible. It won't be easy and won't happen overnight, but it will be worth it.

Your healing journey begins now. Let's take the first step together.

## Reflection Questions:

1. How has betrayal impacted you emotionally, mentally, physically, and spiritually? Be specific and honest in your reflection.

2. What reservations or fears do you have about the idea of forgiveness? What might be holding you back?

3. What do you hope to gain from reading this book? Set an intention for your healing journey.

4. What have you been taught about forgiveness? In my experience, many people don't forgive largely because they don't know what forgiveness is.

# Part I: Understanding Forgiveness

---

# Chapter One

# What is Forgiveness?

"It's about letting go of the bitterness eating us. By giving an unwarranted gift to someone who doesn't deserve it, we find paradoxically that it is we, ourselves, who are freed from that bondage."~Charlotte Witvliet, Ph.D

When Olivia discovered that her husband, James, had been engaging in an online affair, she was devastated. The man she had trusted and loved for over a decade had been secretly exchanging explicit messages and photos with women he met on social media. Olivia felt utterly betrayed, her self-esteem shattered. As she grappled with the pain and confusion, well-meaning friends and family offered advice: "Just forgive him and move on." But what did that even mean? How could she possibly "forgive" such a violation of trust? In her mind, the offense replayed repeatedly. She was so stuck in the past that she was unavailable to James and saw no future for them.

Olivia's struggle to understand forgiveness is a common one. The concept of forgiveness, especially in the context of infidelity, is often misunderstood and oversimplified. It's not uncommon for people to equate forgiveness with forgetting, condoning, or letting the offender off the hook. But true forgiveness is none of these things.

Forgiveness deals with the negative emotions which result from an injustice/offense, whether real or perceived. It is <u>an internal action/decision,</u> while the injustice/offense is <u>external behavior</u>. At its core, forgiveness is a decision to release negative feelings toward the person who hurt you. It's a choice to let go of anger, bitterness, and resentment and to cultivate understanding, empathy, and compassion instead. Forgiveness is not about forgetting the offense or pretending it didn't happen. It's not about excusing or minimizing the hurtful behavior. And it's certainly not about instantly restoring trust or returning to "business as usual" in the relationship. Forgiveness also is not about letting anyone "off the hook" or denying the need for justice.

Rather, forgiveness is about freeing yourself from the toxic grip of unforgiveness and grievances. When we hold onto anger and resentment, it's like drinking poison and expecting the other person to die. Our negative emotions only hurt us, robbing us of peace, joy, and healing. Forgiveness, on the other hand, allows us to release those burdens and reclaim our lives. It also allows us to move from the past to the present and future.

It's important to understand that forgiveness is a process, not a one-time event. It's not something that happens overnight, and it's not always a linear journey. With many people, there is a giving and taking back that happens. There will be setbacks, relapses into anger and bitterness, and days when forgiveness feels impossible. That's okay. What matters is the overall trajectory - a commitment to doing the hard work of letting go and finding peace. With genuine forgiveness, there is also an element of gratitude.

One of the most common misconceptions about forgiveness is that it requires reconciliation. Many people believe that if they forgive their spouse, they must stay in the marriage and restore the relationship. But this simply isn't true. Forgiveness and reconciliation are two separate processes.

Forgiveness is an internal journey that happens within you, while reconciliation is a process between two people that requires the participation and trustworthiness of both partners.

It's entirely possible to forgive your spouse without reconciling the marriage. This was the case for Sophie, who discovered her husband Liam's long-term affair with a close family friend. While Sophie worked hard to forgive Liam and release her anger, she ultimately decided that the marriage was not salvageable due to Liam's lack of remorse and unwillingness to take responsibility for his actions. Sophie forgave him, but she also divorced and created a new life for herself.

On the flip side, it's also possible to reconcile without fully forgiving. This is often the case in the early stages of affair recovery when couples decide to stay together and work on the marriage, even though forgiveness is still a work in progress. The key here is that both partners are committed to the healing process and actively working toward rebuilding trust and intimacy.

As you navigate your own journey of forgiveness, it's important to remember that forgiveness is ultimately a gift you give yourself. It's not about letting your spouse off the hook or condoning their behavior. It's about freeing yourself from the pain and bitterness that will otherwise keep you stuck. Forgiveness is a choice to heal, reclaim your life, and create a future that is not defined by betrayal.

In the coming chapters, we'll explore the benefits, barriers, and practical strategies for letting go and finding peace. But for now, I invite you to reflect on your own understanding of forgiveness and how it might apply to your situation.

## Reflection Questions:

1. What beliefs or misconceptions about forgiveness have you held in the past? How have these beliefs impacted your ability to forgive?

Here are some of the misconceptions about forgiveness:

-Some have taken the general meaning of a frequently used term in the New Testament and Greek language, "aphiemi," which simply means to let go. They believe that is all there is to it, now just do it.

-Another myth, espoused by David Augsburger, states that forgiveness involves restoring trust and letting go of all negative emotions related to the issue. Such a myth adds abuse to abuse victims.

-Still another, as presented in the Anchor Bible Dictionary, summarizes forgiveness as a wiping out of an offense from memory.

2. What would it mean for you to forgive your spouse? What would forgiveness look like in your situation?

3. How might forgiveness (or lack thereof) impact your own well-being and healing process?

4. What are some of the things you tell yourself to keep you from forgiving?

Forgiveness is a deeply personal journey with no one-size-fits-all timeline or approach. Give yourself grace as you navigate this process, and know that healing is possible, one step at a time.

# Chapter Two

# The Benefits of Forgiveness

"Couples who actively practice forgiveness have stronger and healthier relationships."
~John Gottman

When Rachel first discovered her husband Tom's affair, the idea of forgiveness felt impossible. How could she ever forgive such a devastating betrayal? Wouldn't forgiveness mean she was letting Tom off the hook or condoning his behavior? These common fears and misconceptions kept Rachel in anger and bitterness for months.

But as Rachel began to learn more about forgiveness, she discovered that it wasn't about Tom at all—it was about her. She was the one who wasn't sleeping at night and obsessing over what happened. Forgiveness was a choice she could make for her own well-being and healing, regardless of Tom's actions or attitude. As Rachel took tentative steps toward forgiveness, she began to experience firsthand the profound benefits of letting go.

One of the most immediate benefits Rachel noticed was decreased negative emotions. The anger, resentment, and bitterness that had been consuming her began to lose their grip. While the pain of the betrayal was still present, it no longer dominated her every waking moment. Rachel could experience moments of peace, joy, and even hope - emotions that had felt out of reach for so long.

This shift in emotional state had a ripple effect on Rachel's mental and physical health. The constant stress and turmoil of unforgiveness had taken a toll on her body, manifesting in headaches, digestive issues, and insomnia. As Rachel released the negativity, she noticed improved sleep, energy levels, and overall sense of well-being. She felt like she was finally coming up for air after being trapped underwater.

Forgiveness also profoundly impacted Rachel's relationships with Tom and others in her life. As she worked to let go of her anger and bitterness, Rachel could communicate with Tom from a place of greater calm and clarity. She was able to express her hurt and needs without getting lost in explosive arguments or passive-aggressive jabs. This shift created a new dynamic in their relationship, one where healing and understanding could begin to take root.

Rachel's journey of forgiveness also improved her relationships outside the marriage. During the months following the affair, Rachel had become increasingly isolated, pulling away from friends and family. Her bitterness and negativity made connecting with others or finding joy in social interactions difficult. As Rachel released those burdens, she became more present and engaged with loved ones. She rekindled friendships, found support in her community, and even developed new connections with others who had navigated similar experiences.

Perhaps most importantly, forgiveness allowed Rachel to reclaim her sense of self. In the wake of the affair, Rachel's identity had become consumed by victimhood and pain. She had lost sight of who she was beyond the betrayal. But as she chose to forgive, Rachel rediscovered her strength, resilience, and inherent worth. She started pursuing hobbies and passions that had fallen by the wayside, setting boundaries in her relationships, and prioritizing her self-care. Forgiveness allowed Rachel to define herself and her future on her terms.

As you reflect on your situation, it's important to recognize that forgiveness is not a magic wand that will instantly erase all pain or restore broken relationships. Forgiveness is a process, and the benefits often unfold gradually over time. There may be days when anger and hurt resurface, and that's okay. Healing is not a linear journey.

As you take steps toward forgiveness, know that you are not only choosing to release the past - you are choosing a brighter, more peaceful future. You choose emotional freedom, improved health and relationships, and a reclaimed sense of self. No matter the challenges, you choose to heal, grow, and thrive.

Charlotte Witvliet, Ph.D., associate professor of psychology at Hope College, Holland, Michigan says, *"Our research shows that simply thinking about one's offender in a begrudging way can have immediate physical ramifications. Short, fleeting thoughts are unlikely to have a long-term health impact, but we know hostility is a potent risk factor for heart disease. When we have deep wounds, and hostility becomes an ingrained personality trait, then it can be health-eroding."*

Furthermore, a study at Johns Hopkins found that unforgiveness contributes to diabetes and heart disease. When holding onto grudges damages your health you want to consider if it is worth it.

**Consequences of Unforgiveness**

**Physical Consequences**

- **Chemical imbalances (hormones and neurotransmitters)**

Resentment causes an imbalance in the hormones produced by the various glands of the body, producing many physical symptoms and diseases. The longer the unforgiveness, the greater the damage done by the hormones and chemicals released. The chemicals released include hormones and neurotransmitters, both of which influence mood, behavior, thinking, and body functioning.

- **Weakens immune system**

The stress of bitterness/unforgiveness weakens the immune system and heightens one's susceptibility to physical ailments. Often, doctors can trace physical disorders to a point in time when bitterness began to develop. When cortisol levels increase, unforgiveness turns into bitterness.

Unforgiveness increases the risk of heart attack, higher blood pressure, and a slowed digestive system, which can lead to physical symptoms and difficulty thinking.

61 percent of cancer patients have forgiveness issues, and of those, more than half are severe, according to research by Dr. Michael Barry, a board-certified breast oncology surgeon at Margaret West Comprehensive Breast Center in West Cancer Center and Research Institute.

- **Diminished attractiveness**

Refusal to forgive causes fatigue and loss of sleep. Soon, your eyes and facial features reflect your inner distress.

**Mental and Emotional Consequences**
- **Depression**

It takes emotional energy to maintain a grudge. When your emotional energy is exhausted, you become depressed. Unforgiveness can trigger depression or make it worse.

- **Stress**

Hating someone produces what is known as the 'stress hormone' (Cortisol) in your body. You become worn out and unable to cope with daily challenges. Cortisol and other chemicals strain your body and its systems, including the circulatory, digestive, pulmonary, and musculature systems.

- **Disrupts your emotional focus (Your emotional focus changes)**

Bitterness and resentment create an emotional focus toward the person who offended you. This focus causes you to become like the one you resent. The more you think about their actions, the more you reflect on the basic attitudes that prompted them.

Some researchers have uncovered a higher risk of paranoid thinking associated with unforgiveness.

# Reflection Questions:

1. In what ways has unforgiveness impacted your emotional, mental, and physical well-being? What negative effects have you noticed?

2. How might forgiveness improve your relationships - with your spouse, family, friends, and yourself?

3. What positive changes do you hope to see in your life due to choosing forgiveness? What would emotional freedom and healing look like for you?

Forgiveness is not about forgetting the past or excusing hurtful behavior. It's about choosing to release the burdens of anger and bitterness so you can create a future of peace, healing, and joy. The benefits of forgiveness are waiting for you - all you have to do is take the first step.

# Chapter Three

# Barriers to Forgiveness

"We all agree that forgiveness is a beautiful idea until we have to practice it." ~ C.S. Lewis

When Mark discovered his wife Lisa's affair, he was consumed by a whirlwind of emotions - shock, anger, despair, and confusion. As the weeks turned into months, Mark was stuck in a cycle of negativity, rehashing the details of the betrayal and fantasizing about ways to make Lisa pay for what she'd done. Despite his best efforts, Mark couldn't seem to move past the pain and anger. The idea of forgiveness felt not only impossible but unappealing.

Mark's struggle is a common one for those who have experienced infidelity. While forgiveness offers a path to healing and peace, numerous barriers can make the process feel daunting or even undesirable. These barriers can be emotional, psychological, and practical, and they can keep individuals stuck in a cycle of unforgiveness for months or even years.

One of the most significant barriers to forgiveness is fear. Many people worry that forgiving their spouse will make them vulnerable to further hurt or betrayal. They may fear that forgiveness means condoning the affair, letting their partner "off the hook," or losing their right to feel angry and hurt. These fears can be especially potent if the offending spouse has a history of repeated betrayals or has shown little remorse or willingness to change.

Another common barrier is pride. Holding onto our righteous anger and indignation can feel satisfying when we've been deeply hurt. We may believe that forgiveness means weakening our position, admitting defeat, or letting our spouse "win." This pride can be fueled by a sense of moral superiority or a desire for vengeance, both of which can make forgiveness feel like a bitter pill to swallow.

Confusion and misconceptions about forgiveness can also prevent people from letting go. Many people equate forgiveness with forgetting, believing they must act as if the affair never happened in order to truly forgive. Others may think that forgiveness requires immediate reconciliation or a complete restoration of trust. These misunderstandings can create pressure and frustration, making the process of forgiveness seem impossible or unappealing.

Practical barriers, such as ongoing deception or lack of remorse from the offending spouse, can also make forgiveness difficult. If the unfaithful partner is still engaging in the affair, lying, or minimizing the impact of their actions, it can be challenging for the betrayed spouse to find genuine forgiveness. Similarly, forgiveness can feel one-sided and unsatisfying if the offending spouse refuses to take responsibility or make amends.

There are also people who hold onto unforgiveness since it makes you look like a failure. You may be able to live with their failure, but it becomes unforgivable when it casts you in a bad light.

You may also believe that punishing the cheater for what they did is up to you. You may also struggle with wanting to punish yourself for either past bad decisions or for what you perceive as your role in the situation. It is possible that you firmly believe that someone has to punish them and you are the avenger of the offense.

You may consider the offense so great that forgiving them is impossible. Although the offense was great, allowing it to produce bitterness ends up doing more damage to you than the offense itself.

You may believe that the offender must ask for forgiveness before considering it. In such cases, it helps to consider who is suffering, you or the offender? Is holding onto the offense worth the misery it brings?

Finally, unresolved trauma or past hurts can create additional roadblocks on the path to forgiveness. For individuals who have experienced betrayal, abuse, or neglect in the past, the pain of infidelity can trigger deep-seated wounds and fears. Forgiveness can feel impossible or even threatening without addressing and healing these underlying issues.

As you reflect on your own barriers to forgiveness, it's essential to approach these obstacles with self-compassion and patience. Remember that forgiveness is a process, not a singular event. Acknowledging and validating your fears, doubts, and conflicting emotions is okay. Letting go of anger and resentment can be scary, especially when the future feels uncertain.

At the same time, it's important to challenge the beliefs and misconceptions that may keep you stuck. Forgiveness is not about forgetting, condoning, or instantly restoring trust. It's about choosing to release the pain of the past so that you can heal and move forward. Forgiveness does not mean you must reconcile with your spouse or abandon your boundaries and self-respect.

If you struggle with barriers to forgiveness, know that you are not alone. Seeking support from a therapist, counselor, or support group can provide valuable guidance and validation as you navigate this challenging terrain. Remember, the goal is not to achieve perfect forgiveness overnight but rather to take small, consistent steps toward releasing anger and finding peace.

## Reflection Questions:

1. What fears, doubts or misconceptions keep you from embracing forgiveness? How might you challenge or reframe these beliefs?

2. Are there practical barriers, such as ongoing deception or lack of remorse from your spouse, that are making forgiveness difficult? How might you address these challenges or set appropriate boundaries?

3. How might unresolved pain or trauma from your past be impacting your ability to forgive? What steps can you take to heal and address these underlying wounds?

4. Consider listing the offense or offenses and your reason for not forgiving them. What patterns do you see?

Forgiveness is not about letting your spouse off the hook or sacrificing your well-being. It's about freeing yourself from the burden of anger and bitterness to create a future of healing, peace, and joy. By acknowledging and addressing the barriers to forgiveness, you take a powerful step toward reclaiming your life and well-being.

# Chapter Four

# Common Mistakes with Asking for Forgiveness

"Unforgiveness is like drinking poison yourself and waiting for the other person to die."
~Marianne Williamson

Y ou will get the best results dealing with forgiveness issues in person or by phone because it is done when you finish the call or conversation. Contrast this with when it is put down in writing, email, or text messages. Those communications often fall into the wrong hands or stick around much longer than you want them to. Each time the party who has been hurt reads the communication, it can lead to them feeling re-injured again. The hurt party may also share them with others. If there is any possibility or threat of divorce, <u>do not</u> put forgiveness issues in writing. You may be a great communicator, yet when what you wrote is in the hands of a lawyer or in front of a jury, it often hurts you badly. Do not make a video of it, either. Do not deal with forgiveness matters in any way other than verbally over the phone or in person.

An added problem with writing, email, and text messages is that such methods do not always convey the emotions behind your asking for forgiveness. When forgiveness is sought via phone or in person, there are many emotional cues in your tone of voice, eye contact, verbal inflections, and other non-verbal signals. Written communications do not convey those signals, which are often an important part of the communication message. It is hard to convey heartfelt remorse using writing. Although you may have good writing ability, it does not mean you can convey heartfelt emotions.

Those heartfelt emotions are important. Spouses want and need to know that you still need them and feel connected to them. Your spouse will also know if you are using canned words that you picked up from some book or whether they are from your heart. They know how you talk and express yourself. When they hear terms and words from your mouth that you don't typically use, they know that you are using canned words or just 'going through the motions.' They will view you as 'acting.'

The lack of heartfelt emotions and using canned words are also indicative of a weak effort at forgiveness. Your spouse knows that you are following a recipe rather than feeling genuine remorse.

Weak efforts at seeking forgiveness create problems. Although you followed the formula, saying and doing the right thing, any asking for forgiveness is suspect if your heart was not in it. Your spouse may see through such a half-hearted, weak effort. The danger comes when you do not see through your own actions. In such situations, you make a weak effort to seek forgiveness and call it forgiveness. In your mind, you did all you were supposed to. You just don't understand or want to accept your spouse's reaction to your efforts. When your spouse rejects your asking for forgiveness under such circumstances, they see that you are not serious about it.

Written communication also allows you to avoid any kind of personal vulnerability or risk. If your spouse does not feel listened to, using written communication will only alienate them further. Your intentions may be good, but "how" you are doing it makes things worse. When asking for forgiveness in person, questions that create discomfort or emotionally put you on the spot could be asked. In-person communication makes you vulnerable. It also means you can be interrupted.

Within those vulnerable times, interruptions are often opportunities to turn your relationship around. There are risks of vulnerability, yet there is also greater potential for healing when you do it in person. When you ask for forgiveness in person, there is a greater potential for a dialogue and discussion about the hurtful incidents. Your spouse may correct you on what they experienced or talk more about how much it impacted them. When seeking forgiveness, you must stop and listen to what they tell you, even if it is mid-sentence. When you are willing to hear them out and discuss the situation, there are opportunities for healing to occur. You are being tested. If you get defensive, you lose. If you don't allow them to speak, you lose. You lose if you shut them out or dismiss what they tell you. Even under the best circumstances, you may be forgiven with written communication, yet miss out on opportunities to repair your marriage.

Using written communication also allows the offended person to avoid dealing with the issue. They often can pick and choose when they take action, if ever. Written communications regarding forgiveness keeps distance in the relationship. When you ask for forgiveness in person or over the phone, you involve personal risk, forcing the offended person to deal with the situation. While the distance issue makes writing the best way to break off the affair, it is best done in person when it comes to repairing relationships.

Using written communication may allow you to get what you want to say out. Although it gives you the chance to communicate a message without interruption, it is a disrespectful way to interact with your spouse. It is a soft, easy way out of dealing with an important matter that needs to be dealt with face to face. You may be looking for soft, easy ways out and consider doing it in person as scary, but at the same time, it is showing them respect. It's treating them with the dignity they deserve. This is your spouse. This is the bone of your bone, the flesh of your flesh that you married, and you need to treat them with respect and dignity. Even though it's unpleasant, it's important to do it.

Another pitfall to look out for is forgiving too early. Forgiving too early is a problem because when you're in pain, you need a clear understanding of what that pain is about and a clear idea of what it is that you're forgiving. Sometimes you have to let the pain have its perfect work, what the pain does is what it needs to do in your life. Forgiving too early solely to reduce your pain level can lead to emotional confusion and premature closure of significant issues.

Many spouses operate under the assumption that once the issues are forgiven, they are closed for further discussion. If you are married to someone who believes that when the issue is forgiven, it is closed, you will not want to forgive before all the issues important to you are resolved. It would be nice if forgiveness was not linked in such a manner to closure, yet not all spouses think or operate that way.

Premature closure can also occur when you attempt to give blanket forgiveness before you are fully aware of all the issues involved. It is not wise to forgive someone before you know what happened. Forgiveness is not just about you. It is about them as well. Although you may have let go of the issues, they may need to address them as part of their working through them.

Forgiving too early or 'premature closure' is often motivated by wanting to avoid pain, whether the cheater or the betrayed spouse. Our society is used to taking pain relievers to avoid pain. Pain is avoided on many levels in society. The tendency to avoid pain often interferes with the process of forgiveness. Experiencing the discomfort of pain is an essential part of the forgiveness process. Pain is a motivator. Removing it reduces the level of motivation for change. Many people do not understand the benefits of pain and how forgiving too soon stops the pain from doing what it needs to do as part of the forgiveness process.

Take Jane and Joe, for example. If Jane forgives Joe too early, then Joe never has to face his own pain associated with his affair. Not only does he not face the pain, but the 'premature closure' stops his conscience from developing to the maturity it needs to. The cheater needs pain to mold and shape their conscience because if they are going to make a heartfelt plea for forgiveness because they feel like what they've done is wrong, they need to have the emotional pain of their conscience kick in. The conscience does not kick in, jump start, or whatever you want to call it until the amount of pain they feel reaches a critical level. When the pain reaches a critical level, people take action.

Ideally, Jane would want Joe's plea for forgiveness to be the result of Joe's conscience. It is better if the plea for forgiveness is driven by his conscience and not because Jane is putting him on guilt trips, playing his holy spirit, or whatever else she may be doing to try to induce the guilt. You want the pain and guilt to come from inside of him rather than be from outside nagging. Jane should want him to have remorse for what he did and ask for forgiveness for it.

Letting your spouse's pain build up is not easy. It is hard to sit back and let your spouse squirm in discomfort, but the discomfort is an important part of their growth and forgiveness process.

When you forgive too early, you are fuzzy on what you're forgiving, and your action can stop the cheater's conscience from doing what it needs to. Besides the conscience, forgiving too early can stunt other emotional maturity and growth in the relationship. Sometimes, allowing the pain to sink in is the best thing that you can do, but that requires some maturity and allowing your spouse to be hurt for a little while. This is where you have to look at the long-term benefit rather than the short-term discomfort.

Pain means something is wrong, and you need to take care of it. You go to the doctor to get out of pain. In many cases, pain motivates us, and when you forgive too early, you take away the motivation provided by the pain.

## Reflection Questions:

1. Have you ever sought forgiveness through written communication? How did it impact the outcome, and what might you do differently in the future?

2. Reflect on a time when you forgave someone too early. What were the consequences, and how did it affect your emotional growth and the relationship?

3. How can you practice vulnerability and emotional depth when seeking forgiveness in person? What steps can you take to prepare yourself for these challenging conversations?

4. In what ways has pain served as a motivator for change and growth in your life? How can you apply this understanding to the forgiveness process in your relationship?

5. How can you balance the need for forgiveness with the importance of allowing pain to serve its purpose? What signs might indicate that you or your partner are ready to genuinely seek or grant forgiveness?

# Part II: The Forgiveness Process

Restore The Family Press

# Chapter Five

# Preparing to Forgive

When Jessica first learned of her husband Brian's infidelity, she felt like her world had shattered. The trust, love, and security she had built her life upon had been ripped away in an instant. As Jessica grappled with the tidal wave of emotions - rage, despair, confusion, and shame - the idea of forgiveness felt like a distant and impossible dream.

But as the weeks passed, Jessica began to realize that holding onto her anger and bitterness was only causing her more pain. She was the one in misery, not Brian. She knew that if she wanted to heal and move forward, forgiveness would have to be part of her journey. The question was, where to begin?

If you find yourself in a similar situation, know that forgiveness requires preparation and intentionality. Before you can truly let go and forgive, there are several key steps you can take to lay the groundwork for healing.

The first step is to acknowledge the pain and impact of the affair. This may seem obvious, but it's not uncommon for individuals to minimize or deny the extent of their hurt in an attempt to cope or move on quickly. However, true forgiveness cannot happen without first fully acknowledging and validating the pain you have experienced. You must clearly understand what you are forgiving and the associated emotions before forgiving.

Take time to sit with your emotions, even the uncomfortable or scary ones. Journal about your experiences, talk to a trusted friend, pastor, or therapist, or simply allow yourself to feel the full weight of your grief and anger. Acknowledging the impact of the betrayal is not about wallowing in victimhood but rather about honoring your pain and giving yourself permission to heal.

As you process your emotions, practicing self-care and self-compassion is essential. Infidelity can take a tremendous toll on your physical, emotional, and mental well-being. Make sure to prioritize activities that bring you joy, relaxation, and comfort. This might include exercise, time in nature, creative hobbies, or connecting with supportive loved ones.

It's also crucial to extend compassion and kindness toward yourself. Betrayal can stir up intense feelings of self-doubt, shame, and inadequacy. Remember that your partner's actions do not reflect your worth or lovability. Their having the affair does not mean you are a failure. Practice speaking to yourself with the same gentleness and understanding you would offer a dear friend.

Another key step in preparing to forgive is to educate yourself about the process. Many people have misconceptions or unrealistic expectations about what forgiveness entails. They may believe forgiveness means forgetting the betrayal, condoning the behavior, or instantly restoring trust and intimacy.

Forgiveness starts with releasing the anger, resentment, and bitterness that keep you trapped in pain. It's about choosing to let go of the past so that you can heal and move forward. Forgiveness does not mean forgetting, excusing, or necessarily reconciling with your partner.

Take time to read books and articles or attend workshops on the topic of forgiveness. Learn from the experiences of others who have navigated this challenging path. By understanding what forgiveness is (and isn't), you can approach the process with greater clarity and realistic expectations.

As you prepare to forgive, it's also important to set boundaries and prioritize your own healing. Forgiveness does not mean tolerating ongoing disrespect, deception, or abuse. If your partner is still engaging in hurtful behaviors or refusing to take responsibility for their actions, it may not be safe or healthy to move forward with deeper levels of forgiveness.

In these cases, it's essential to prioritize your own well-being and establish clear boundaries around what you will and will not tolerate. If there are safety issues, this might mean separating from your partner, seeking legal guidance, or limiting contact until they demonstrate genuine commitment to change.

Remember, forgiveness is ultimately a choice you make for yourself, not for your partner. It's about reclaiming your power, peace, and joy, regardless of your partner's actions or attitude. Your forgiving them does not hinge on their actions or attitudes.

As you take steps to prepare for forgiveness, be patient and compassionate with yourself. The journey of healing is rarely predictable. There will be setbacks, challenges, and moments of doubt. But by laying the groundwork of self-awareness, self-care, education, and boundary-setting, you are equipping yourself with the tools and resilience needed to navigate this path.

Trust that forgiveness is possible, even if it feels out of reach right now. By taking small, consistent steps toward releasing anger and finding peace, you are moving closer to the freedom and healing your heart desires.

## Reflection Questions:

1. What emotions have you been minimizing or avoiding in the wake of the affair? How might acknowledging and validating these feelings support your healing process?

2. What self-care practices can you incorporate into your daily routine to support your physical, emotional, and mental well-being?

3. What boundaries do you need to establish with your partner (or ex-partner) to prioritize your own healing and safety? How can you communicate these boundaries clearly and assertively? Start by writing them down, beginning with "I will..." or "I will not..." to make them clear and firm.

Preparing to forgive is not about rushing the process or forcing yourself to "get over" the pain. It's about creating a foundation of self-awareness, self-compassion, and self-protection that will allow you to approach forgiveness from a place of strength and clarity. Trust your timeline, honor your unique needs, and know that healing is possible, one step at a time.

# Chapter Six

# Letting Go

When Adam first discovered his wife Sarah's infidelity, he felt like he was drowning in a sea of anger, betrayal, and despair. The pain was so intense that it felt physical, like a crushing weight on his chest that made it hard to breathe. For months, Adam was consumed by thoughts of revenge, obsessing over ways to make Sarah pay for what she had done. He believed she needed to be punished for what she did.

However, as time passed, Adam began to realize that his anger and bitterness were only causing him more suffering. He felt trapped in a cycle of negativity, unable to move forward or find any sense of peace. Deep down, Adam knew that if he wanted to heal and reclaim his life, he would need to find a way to let go of the pain and resentment that were holding him hostage.

If you are in a similar situation, know that letting go is the next critical step toward forgiveness. It's a process of releasing the anger, hurt, and resentment that keep you trapped in the past and prevent you from healing and moving forward. While letting go can feel scary or impossible at first, there are concrete strategies and tools you can use to begin the process.

One powerful tool for letting go is visualization. Close your eyes and imagine yourself holding onto all the anger, hurt, and betrayal you feel. Picture these emotions as physical objects - perhaps a heavy rock, a tangled knot, or a dark cloud. Take a few deep breaths, and then imagine yourself setting these objects down. Watch as they drift away from you, getting smaller and smaller until they disappear. Allow yourself to feel the lightness and relief of releasing these burdens.

It is also important to make a conscious choice to start the letting go process. Making that choice requires an act of the will. You choose to let go, even though you may not feel like it or want to.

## The Who, What, When, Where, and How of Forgiveness

When I attended High School in the 1970s, I was fascinated with journalism and was on the school newspaper staff. One of the lessons they drilled into young journalists then was that a news story must give the 'Who, What, When, & Where' of what it reported. In some cases, you could include the Why and How.

### -Who

This is a great place to start since, with forgiveness, you forgive people – the Who.

When you decide to forgive, you need a clear idea of 'Who' is being forgiven. When you are faced with the pain of an affair, there are many people involved and many wrongs. When your feelings are raw, you can take offense to many things.

With an affair, the one you need to consider is the cheater. It is the cheater that's forgiven, not the cheating. You want to make peace with the person, not what they did. This means that you forgive the cheater.

To forgive the cheater requires you to separate 'who' they are from 'what' they did. This separation is hard when you are not used to doing it. You do not want a relationship with the behavior; you want your spouse back. For that reason, you don't forgive the behavior; you forgive the person.

When forgiveness happens, it's as if the walls and barriers that kept the two of you apart are removed. The barrier that kept the two of you away from each other begins to crumble away.

You can choose to forgive the lover and others involved, yet the main priority is your spouse.

When you start separating out who they are from what they did, the experience gets very real. In order to help your mind grasp what is going on, write down what they did. In some cases, you may also want to include what they didn't do but should have done as well. (example: You may have wanted them to delete their Facebook friends. When they didn't do it, that experience troubled you).

If what they did or didn't do caused you problems, those items need to be written down.

**-What**

Forgiving also involves letting go of negative emotional states and tension. These include anger, bitterness, resentment, the desire for revenge, sadness, and many others.

When you choose the forgiveness option, you'll need to identify and write down all those negative emotional states you have been experiencing. Identifying them and writing them down are crucial steps in forgiving. Your mind needs to know what your heart has been struggling with, and writing this down allows your brain and heart to connect.

The more specific you can be in identifying them, the better. One common mistake in forgiving is that the injured party is not clear on what negative emotional states they are experiencing. Choosing to forgive BEFORE you have a clear idea of what you're experiencing can set you up for continued negative episodes, free-floating anxiety, and continued tension.

In such cases, you may find yourself saying, "I forgave them for ___________, so why am I still feeling this way?" This means that you were not specific in identifying those negative emotional states you've been struggling with.

If you are uncomfortable admitting your anger, this part of forgiving may be a struggle for you. You'll need tough 'emotional honesty.' This means that if you have experienced suicidal or homicidal thoughts and feelings, you'll need to admit this to yourself. When it comes time for forgiving, censoring what you write down or toning down what you feel will limit the benefits of forgiving. This list also helps when using the visualization approach.

When I conducted the Affair Recovery Survey, roughly 10-15% of those responding admitted having such feelings after an affair. Since an affair is very personal, it's often taken very personally. Often, the degree to which you were hurt is the degree to which you want to hurt.

When you start facing the hurts associated with forgiveness, the feelings may be intense at times, both with you and the betrayer. There may even be a risk of violence. That risk is higher if there has already been violence in your marriage.

Safety is always a priority, even when it comes to forgiveness issues. Being honest and bringing up issues associated with forgiveness is important, yet when it puts you or your spouse in danger of physical or emotional harm, the priority is safety.

When intense feelings of anger are aroused, there is a risk that you or your spouse will lash out in reaction. The affair is already evidence that at least one person has weak impulse control. Combining weak impulse control and intense anger is a dangerous combination.

If your anger is intense enough to hurt yourself or others, or your spouse's anger is that intense, those issues will need attention prior to forgiveness.

Forgiveness can trigger intense anger. Any action that has transformative power also has the power to trigger strong reactions, positive or negative.

### -When

The simple answer to the question, 'When to forgive?' is 'When you are tired of hurting.' In its truest sense, forgiveness is about letting go of painful and hurtful feelings. The one who benefits most from forgiveness is you.

Although it helps when the betrayer approaches you and asks for forgiveness, that is not a required pre-requisite. You can forgive them without them asking for it. This is because forgiveness is about you letting go of things rather than them confessing matters to you and asking you for forgiveness.

It also helps to have a clear idea of what forgiveness concerns. The clearer you are about the forgiveness concerns, the deeper the healing you experience. Each day of carrying the pain and negative thoughts costs you. Whether in terms of your peace of mind, your stress level, or the amount of space in your mind, the betrayer takes over.

You can put off forgiveness or even choose not to forgive. The downside of that choice is that you will experience the consequences of unforgiveness.

It's also important to cultivate self-compassion and forgiveness towards yourself. When we've been betrayed, it's common to turn our anger and blame inward, criticizing ourselves for not seeing the signs or preventing the affair. But holding onto self-blame and shame only keeps us stuck in the past and prevents us from healing.

Practice speaking to yourself with kindness and understanding, as you would a friend going through a similar situation. Remind yourself that you are not responsible for your partner's choices and that you deserve love, respect, and healing. By extending forgiveness and compassion to yourself, you create a foundation of self-love and acceptance that makes it easier to let go of anger toward others.

Focusing on the present moment and the future you want to create is important as you work on letting go. When we're trapped in anger and resentment, our energy and attention are focused on the past—on what happened, what we lost, and how we were wronged. But by shifting our focus to the present and future, we can begin to envision and create a life that is not defined by betrayal.

Take time to identify your values, goals, and dreams. What kind of life do you want to build for yourself? What brings you joy, meaning, and fulfillment? Focusing on these positive aspirations gives you a roadmap for healing and growth. You remind yourself that your story doesn't end with the affair - that you have the power to create a new chapter of resilience, strength, and joy.

It's important to remember that letting go is not a one-time event but rather an ongoing practice. There will be days when anger and resentment resurface, and that's okay. Healing is not straightforward, and setbacks are a normal part of the journey. What matters is that you continue to commit to the process of releasing and forgiving, even when it feels difficult or impossible.

One helpful way to maintain this commitment is to surround yourself with supportive people who can offer encouragement, validation, and accountability. This might include friends, family members, a therapist, or a support group for those who have experienced infidelity. By sharing your journey with others who understand and support your healing, you remind yourself that you are not alone and that forgiveness is possible.

As you take steps to let go of anger and resentment, celebrate your progress and successes, no matter how small. Acknowledge the moments when you choose forgiveness over bitterness, extend compassion to yourself or others, and focus on the present and future rather than the past. These moments are evidence of your strength, resilience, and capacity for healing.

Remember, letting go is not about condoning or forgetting the betrayal. Forgiveness is about choosing to release the pain and anger that keep you trapped so you can create a future of freedom, peace, and joy. By committing to the practice of letting go, you open yourself up to new possibilities for healing, growth, and love.

## Reflection Questions:

1. What specific emotions, thoughts, or memories do you need to let go of to move forward on your healing journey?

2. What self-care practices can you engage in to cultivate self-compassion and forgiveness towards yourself?

3. How can you shift your focus from the past to the present and future? What goals, dreams, or aspirations can you focus on to create a life of meaning and fulfillment?

Letting go is a courageous and powerful act of self-love and self-preservation. It's a declaration that you deserve to heal, grow, and thrive, no matter your challenges or betrayals. Trust in your own resilience, and know that by releasing the pain of the past, you are creating space for a future of boundless possibility and joy.

# Chapter Seven

# Shifting Perspectives

"Forgive, not because they deserve forgiveness, but because you deserve peace." ~Author unknown

When Emily learned of her husband Juan's affair, she was consumed by feelings of betrayal, anger, and worthlessness. She couldn't understand how Juan could throw away their years of love and commitment for a fleeting infatuation. Emily felt like she would never be able to trust again and that her entire marriage had been a lie.

As Emily struggled to make sense of the affair, she found herself stuck in a cycle of blame, self-doubt, and resentment. She replayed every moment of her marriage, searching for signs she had missed or ways she had fallen short. She vilified Juan, painting him as a selfish monster who had deliberately set out to hurt her. She questioned her own judgment, attractiveness, and lovability.

One day, a friend gently suggested that Emily try to look at the situation from a different perspective. At first, Emily was resistant - how could there be any other way to look at such a devastating betrayal? However, as she reflected on her friend's words, Emily began to realize that her current perspective was only causing her more pain and keeping her stuck in the past.

If you are in a similar situation, know that shifting your perspective is the next step for forgiveness and healing. When we've been betrayed, it's natural to get trapped in a narrow, black-and-white viewpoint that vilifies our partner and victimizes ourselves. You may think that there is only one way of looking at what happened: your way. But by intentionally exploring different perspectives, we can begin to loosen the grip of anger and resentment and create space for understanding, empathy, and release. It amounts to looking at what happened from different angles and considering other narratives explaining the events.

One way to shift perspective is to try to understand your partner's behavior without condoning it. This doesn't mean excusing the affair or absolving your partner of responsibility. Rather, it's about looking at the situation with curiosity and openness, seeking to understand the complex factors that may have contributed to your partner's choices.

This might involve exploring your partner's personal history, unmet needs, or emotional struggles. It could mean examining the dynamics of your relationship and identifying patterns of communication or disconnection that may have left your partner feeling lonely or unfulfilled. It also helps to consider the context of their life in terms of a family history of affairs or traumas they went through. By gaining a more nuanced understanding of the context surrounding the affair, you can begin to see your partner as a flawed, struggling human being rather than a one-dimensional villain.

Another way to shift perspective is to challenge the beliefs and stories you're telling yourself about the affair. In the wake of betrayal, engaging in all-or-nothing thinking is common, such as "my entire marriage was a lie" or "I'll never be able to trust again." But these extreme, absolutist beliefs are rarely accurate or helpful.

Try to catch yourself in these moments of black-and-white thinking and intentionally explore alternative perspectives. For example, instead of telling yourself that your entire marriage was a lie, you might acknowledge the moments of love, connection, and growth that were also part of your relationship. Instead of believing that you'll never trust again, you might remind yourself of your own resilience and capacity for healing.

As you work to shift your perspective, it can also be helpful to focus on your own growth and learning. While the pain of betrayal can be overwhelming, it can also be an opportunity for profound personal transformation. By focusing on your own healing and self-discovery, you can begin to see the affair as a catalyst for positive change rather than a defining moment of devastation.

This might involve exploring your own patterns of communication, boundary-setting, or self-esteem. It could mean rediscovering hobbies, passions, or goals that you had lost sight of during your relationship. By intentionally cultivating a growth mindset and focusing on your own development, you remind yourself that the affair doesn't define you and that you can create a future of healing and resilience.

As you practice shifting perspectives, be patient and compassionate with yourself. Letting go of entrenched beliefs and stories can be challenging, especially when we're in the midst of intense emotional pain. There may be days when you slip back into old thinking patterns, and that's okay. What matters is that you continue intentionally exploring new viewpoints and possibilities, even when it feels difficult or uncomfortable.

Remember, shifting your perspective doesn't mean minimizing or dismissing the pain of the betrayal. It's not about making excuses for your partner or forgiving before you're ready. Rather, it's about creating space for a more nuanced, compassionate understanding of yourself, your partner, and your relationship. It's about recognizing that the story of the affair is not the entire story of your life and that you have the power to write a new chapter of healing, growth, and love.

## Reflection Questions:

1. What beliefs or stories are you telling yourself about the affair that may keep you stuck in anger or resentment? How might you challenge or reframe these beliefs? Is there another way of telling the story?

2. What factors or experiences in your partner's life may have contributed to their decision to have an affair? How might understanding these factors (without excusing the behavior) support your own healing process?

3. How can you focus on your own growth and learning in the aftermath of the affair? What new insights, skills, or strengths do you want to cultivate as you move forward?

Shifting your perspective is a powerful act of self-love and self-empowerment. By intentionally exploring new ways of understanding yourself, your partner, and your experience, you open yourself up to new possibilities for healing, forgiveness, and transformation. Trust in your resilience, and know that you can create a future of hope, joy, and love, no matter what challenges you have faced.

# Chapter Eight

# From Betrayal to Trust: Steps to Rebuilding a Stronger Relationship After Infidelity

"Forgiveness Can't Be Forced. While you have the power to say sorry, the other person has the freedom to forgive or not to forgive." `
Esther Perel

When David's wife Laura confessed to having an affair with her coworker, David felt like his entire world had been turned upside down. The person he trusted most, the one he had built his life around, had lied to him and betrayed their marriage vows. In the days and weeks following the revelation, David grappled with intense feelings of anger, betrayal, and disbelief.

As the initial shock began to subside, David realized that he had a difficult decision to make. Could he find a way to rebuild trust with Laura and salvage their marriage? Or was the betrayal simply too great to overcome? David knew that forgiveness was a crucial first step, but he also recognized that forgiveness alone wouldn't be enough to heal the deep wounds inflicted by the affair.

If you find yourself in a situation similar to David's, it's essential to understand that rebuilding trust after infidelity is a gradual, intentional process. It requires a sincere commitment. Although it works best with involvement from both partners, that does not always happen or happen at the same time.

It also requires a willingness to confront painful truths, establish new boundaries, and cultivate a culture of honesty and transparency.

One of the first steps in rebuilding trust is for the partner who had the affair to take full responsibility for their actions. This means acknowledging the deep pain and betrayal they have caused, expressing genuine remorse, and committing to making amends. It's not enough for the unfaithful partner to simply say, "I'm sorry." They must be willing to engage in the hard work of self-reflection, be honest about what they did and its impact, be consistent, and exhibit trustworthy behavior.

This process of taking responsibility may involve individual or couples therapy, where the unfaithful partner can explore the underlying issues, insecurities, or unmet needs that contributed to their decision to cheat. It may also involve setting clear boundaries around contact with the affair partner, being transparent about whereabouts and communications, and demonstrating a willingness to answer questions and reassure the betrayed partner.

For the betrayed partner, rebuilding trust also requires a willingness to openly express their feelings, needs, and expectations. This can be a challenging and vulnerable process, especially if there is a history of conflict avoidance or communication breakdowns in the relationship. However, the betrayed partner needs to communicate what they need in order to feel safe, respected, and valued in the relationship moving forward. This communication needs to be clear. For example, let them know if you need more time with each other. Let them know if you need them to let you check their phone.

This might involve requesting regular check-ins, setting boundaries around privacy and personal space, or establishing clear consequences for any future breaches of trust. It may also involve working with a therapist or counselor to process the intense emotions triggered by the affair and develop healthy coping strategies.

As both partners work to rebuild trust, it's important to focus on creating a new, stronger foundation for the relationship. This means not only repairing the damage caused by the affair but also addressing any underlying issues or dynamics that may have contributed to the breakdown of trust in the first place.

This might involve learning new ways of talking with each other, learning how to listen without reacting defensively, recognizing that emotions and facts are two separate things, and allowing each other time to answer without interruption. It may mean prioritizing quality time together, rekindling physical and emotional intimacy, and finding new ways to support and appreciate each other. It could also involve setting shared goals, cultivating shared interests and values, and creating a vision for the future of the relationship.

As you navigate the process of rebuilding trust, it's essential to be patient and compassionate with yourself and your partner. What you are forgiving is them, NOT the infidelity or lying. You forgive the person. Healing from infidelity is a deeply personal journey, and there is no one-size-fits-all timeline or approach. There may be setbacks, triggers, and moments of doubt along the way - this is normal and to be expected.

What matters is that both partners remain committed to the process, even when it feels challenging or uncomfortable. This means being willing to have difficult conversations, confront painful truths, and take responsibility for one's own growth and healing. It means prioritizing the relationship and the well-being of both partners, even in the face of fear, uncertainty, or external pressures.

Ultimately, rebuilding trust after infidelity is a testament to the resilience and strength of the human heart. It requires courage, vulnerability, and a deep belief in the power of love and forgiveness. By committing to this process, you and your partner can heal from the wounds of betrayal and create a stronger, more authentic, and more intimately connected than ever.

## Reflection Questions:

1. What specific actions or behaviors must your partner demonstrate to rebuild trust? What boundaries or agreements must you establish to feel safe and respected in the relationship?

2. What unresolved issues or dynamics in your relationship may have contributed to the breakdown of trust? How can you and your partner work together to address these underlying challenges?

3. How can you prioritize self-care and emotional healing as you navigate the process of rebuilding trust? What support systems or resources do you need to cultivate resilience and maintain hope?

Rebuilding trust after infidelity is a courageous and transformative act of love. By committing to this process, you are healing the wounds of the past and creating a foundation for a future of greater honesty, intimacy, and connection. Trust in the journey, lean on your support systems, and know that a stronger, more beautiful relationship is possible with patience, compassion, and dedication.

# Chapter Nine

# The Steps of Forgiveness

Forgiveness is crucial to healing and rebuilding a relationship after an affair. However, the process of forgiveness can be challenging, and it requires a deep understanding of one's emotions and a willingness to let go of the pain and anger associated with the betrayal. This chapter will explore a step-by-step approach to forgiveness that involves acknowledging and releasing the pain, separating the person from their actions, and investing in the relationship moving forward.

The process of forgiveness is not about condoning the affair or minimizing its impact on the betrayed partner. Instead, it is about finding a way to move forward and create a healthier, more resilient relationship. By following the steps outlined in this chapter, you can work towards forgiveness and begin the process of healing and rebuilding trust with your partner.

Step 1—Recall the pain and emotions that you are struggling with. Once they have been brought to your awareness, verbalize them AND write them down. While verbalizing them, show with your hands how painful it was (clenched fists, open hands, one hand slapping the other, etc.). This will help you gain clarity with what you are dealing with. Your body may know about feelings and recall things that your mind may be blocking out.

Step 2—Verbalize the feeling and hand those feelings up as if letting go or releasing them. If you believe in God, lift them up to God by stretching your hand and arm upward. If you want to lift them up to the universe, do so. Use hand motions to lift them up. If you are unsure of where you stand in terms of God, consider lifting them up to the universe. While lifting them upward, say aloud that you are letting go of them. For example, "I am letting go of the anger and nasty bitterness."

Step 3—Verbally rage at the behavior while illustrating the amount of rage that you feel by using your hands. You might say things like, "It shouldn't have happened. It wasn't fair. I didn't deserve it." This step is often very difficult for many people because many of you have been taught not to express extreme anger. After raging, it's important to recognize and acknowledge that there are more ways of looking at the affair than just yours. It's okay if you don't agree with the other perspective; you just need to acknowledge that there's more than one way of looking at what happened. You need to open up the possibility of other ways of looking at the affair than just yours. It often helps verbalize other potential ways of looking at the affair. If you have raging feelings about those perspectives, now is a good time to express them. If you have trouble seeing the affair from any other perspective than yours, it's an indication that there are still some emotional issues that have not been addressed in Steps 1 & 2.

Step 4—Separate the person from what he or she did. Say, "I separate you from what you did," while using your hands and separating them to opposite sides to show you are separating the two things. After separating them from what they did, acknowledge that they had their reasons for doing what they did.

Step 5—Verbalize to YOURSELF that you forgive the person. Again, use your hands to illustrate that forgiveness. This helps cement the forgiveness in your heart and head. Verbalize to yourself how you can demonstrate that you forgive them. **Never** tell someone you forgave him or her unless the person asks for it. This is a time when you give yourself permission for them to 'make it up to you.' Verbalize that you are willing to let them 'make it right.' They may or may not make things right, but this needs to be done to lower defensive walls. When you allow them to 'make it right,' you open up possibilities of reconciliation. Since this is about you letting go of issues, doing this allows you to be more open to them. Before taking this step, you may have been closed off to them. They may have even told you this. When resentments build up, there are also defensive walls that go up as well. This part of the exercise lowers the walls, whether or not you were aware of them being there.

Step 6—The next step is investing in them and allowing for a relationship. You can show it by doing things where you invest in their lives. This includes sending a card or simply calling and telling the person you were thinking about him or her and wondered how he or she was doing. Then, do what you verbalized. If you truly forgive people, you must serve them in some way, like sending a greeting card, a phone call, a small gift, or praying for them. It is best not to expect any appreciation for what is done. This action is important for you and changing your feelings toward the betrayer.

## Reflection Questions:

1. How has holding onto anger and resentment towards your partner affected your emotional well-being and your relationship?

2. What are some of the most challenging aspects of verbalizing and releasing the pain and emotions associated with the affair?

3. How can acknowledging your partner's perspective on the affair, even if you don't agree with it, contribute to the process of forgiveness?

4. In what ways can separating your partner from their actions help you move towards forgiveness and reconciliation?

5. What specific actions can you take to invest in your relationship and demonstrate your forgiveness to your partner?

# Chapter Ten

# Forgiveness Clears the Path: How to Rebuild a Relationship After Infidelity Without Ignoring the Damage

"Forgiveness is about giving yourself the future you deserve – unhampered by hurt and anger."-Gottman Institute

Forgiveness is a crucial step in the healing process after an affair, but it is not the end of the journey. Once forgiveness has been granted, there is still significant work to be done to repair the relationship and rebuild trust. This chapter explores the importance of continued communication, unconditional acceptance, and the need to address the consequences of the affair even after forgiveness has been given.

When there is forgiveness, you will be able to talk and engage with each other. With forgiveness, you have removed the obstacles. The two of you still need to work on what needs repairing in your relationship.

When you forgive, you can accept the cheater unconditionally. Likewise, the cheater can accept you unconditionally. This means that you accept them the way that they are, and you accept them and what they say without any conditions. This does not necessarily mean that the two of you are ready to be back in a relationship, especially if there are safety concerns, which I will deal with later.

The two of you not only accept each other unconditionally but are also able to discuss things without defensiveness or insecurities getting in the way. There will still be some defensiveness and insecurity, but not to the point where it totally blocks or shuts down communication.

One of the misconceptions about forgiveness is the assumption that you're letting the person off the hook. They are not 'off the hook.' Forgiveness is not a pardon. The wrongs still need to be corrected. The damage will need to be repaired. The forgiveness only removed the roadblocks. An illustration of this is that the roads have to be cleared after a disaster, such as a hurricane. Once they are cleared, the survivors can begin repairing the damage and rebuilding what was destroyed. Forgiveness amounts to removing the blockading debris that litters the roads. Forgiving without doing any further work would be like clearing the roads and leaving the damaged areas in a state of neglect.

The cheater may assume that once you have forgiven them, they never have to talk about the affair again. That is not the case. They will still need to talk about the affair along with how it impacted your marriage relationship. There will need to be accountability without the condemnation that comes with unforgiveness.

When you forgive the cheater, it does not mean that you cannot discuss what happened anymore or that you approve of what happened. To illustrate, let us examine the word "pardon," noting what it literally means.

The term itself, the "par," refers to a person. The last half, the "don" part, refers to the debt that the offender owes you, which comes from "dono." "Dono" means 'give for' or 'give,' so essentially, when you pardon somebody, you are giving to the person. The emphasis is on the person and not the behavior. In the case of a pardon, the person is pardoned, NOT the act. Even in the definition of the word 'pardon,' the person is forgiven, NOT what they did.

Another way of putting it is that you are letting go of that debt that they owe you emotionally. You are forgiving that debt. That does not mean that what they did was right. That does not mean you cannot talk about it because you do need to talk about it. You have released them from what they owe you and the sense of obligation that goes with it. Forgiveness emotionally releases the person. They still have an obligation to make up for what they did.

When you forgive, you are forgiving the person and not the action.

The cheater often does not want to talk about the affair and its consequences. There are many reasons for this. One is because it's painful. Nobody likes facing what they did wrong or the pain they caused again and again and again and again. It is understandable to not desire to be reminded of pain and wrongdoing. At the same time, the affair does need to be revisited because it was a shock to the marital relationship. The first few times you go through discussions about the affair, the betrayed spouse is often not hearing everything that is being said to them. You may be a good listener, yet when the affair personally affects you, it impacts your ability to listen to any recounting objectively. When the cheater says something that you disagree with, you may stop listening at that point. They may continue talking, but your mind is looping around your disagreement with them and how to present your point.

It's like an instant replay loop that keeps going over and over and over and over. Each time you go through the loop, a little more sinks in for the betrayed spouse, but they can't fully grasp everything they are being told. Many cheaters will turn around and want forgiveness because they think this means they no longer have to talk about the affair. They may use phrases like "It's behind us", "Let's put this behind us" or "That door is shut!"

With forgiveness, you are back in a relationship with your spouse, but you still have to deal with the affair. Take bankruptcy, for example. Bankruptcy has a big impact on a couple. Even when the bankruptcy is forgiven, there is still a mark on your record. You have to rebuild your credit and your reputation. You still have to deal with it with the credit companies and the consequences of what happened. The creditors are not interested in your motives for bankruptcy. They want to be paid. Whether or not your situation was your fault, you have to deal with it and repair the damage. In the case of bankruptcy, you have to get your financial house in order. In the case of an affair, you have to get your relationship house in order.

With each re-telling of the affair, the narrative changes. It is not a matter of lies and deceit. These changes represent changes in the thinking and emotional awareness of the narrator. It also represents changes in perspective. You want the cheater to consider and incorporate your perspective. The changes in the affair narrative are a marker you can use to track changes in the cheater's thinking.

Forgiveness removes any mental or emotional blockages that keep the narrator or you from completing the narrative. Each re-telling of the narrative allows forgiveness to sink in deeper. For the betrayed spouse, the retelling gives you clarity in terms of understanding your spouse and yourself. For the cheater, each retelling allows the reality of forgiveness to reach deeper into them and their thinking. Although the re-telling does not feel like a win-win at the time, it allows for a deeper connection. When you only forgive and do not repair the relationship and the narrative, it may leave you feeling incomplete, with the distance between you and the cheater still in place.

## Reflection Questions:

1. How can you and your partner work together to repair the damage caused by the affair, even after forgiveness has been granted?

2. How can unconditional acceptance contribute to the healing process and rebuilding trust in your relationship?

3. Why is it important to continue discussing the affair and its consequences, even after forgiveness has been given? How can you approach these conversations in a productive and non-judgmental way?

4. How can you use the changes in the affair narrative as a tool to track your partner's growth and changes in perspective?

5. What steps can you take to ensure that forgiveness leads to a deeper connection and a stronger relationship rather than leaving you feeling incomplete or distant from your partner?

# Part III: Life After Forgiveness

# Chapter Eleven

# Forgiving Yourself

"How unhappy is he who cannot forgive himself!" ~Publilius Syrus, 1st century BCE, from the Latin by D. Lyman, 1856

When Caroline discovered that her husband, Michael, had been having an affair with his ex-girlfriend, she was devastated. The betrayal felt like a physical blow, leaving her reeling with shock, anger, and despair. As Caroline grappled with the fallout of the affair, she found herself consumed not only by rage towards Michael but also by intense feelings of shame, self-doubt, and self-blame.

Caroline couldn't help but question her own role in the breakdown of the marriage. She berated herself for not being attentive enough, for letting herself go, for not being sexy or exciting enough to keep Michael's interest. She replayed every argument, every moment of distance or disconnection, wondering if she could have done something differently to prevent the affair. At times, she ran off and hid in a safe space. Even though it was safe, she had dark thoughts about cutting herself, thinking it would release the pain.

As Caroline struggled to make sense of her own emotions, she realized that one of the biggest barriers to her healing was her inability to forgive herself. She was holding herself to an impossible standard of perfection, blaming herself for another person's choices and actions. She recognized that if she wanted to truly move forward and find peace, she would need to learn to extend compassion and forgiveness to Michael and herself.

If you find yourself in a situation similar to Caroline's, it's important to understand that self-forgiveness is an essential component of healing after infidelity. When we've been betrayed by a partner, it's natural to internalize feelings of shame, inadequacy, and self-doubt. You may blame yourself for not being good enough, not seeing the signs, or somehow causing your partner to stray. Just by viewing it this way, you are holding onto the idea that it was all about your sex appeal or relationship magnetism. Having such a view does not allow your spouse to make choices, be they good or bad.

However, holding onto these feelings of self-blame and self-recrimination only keeps us stuck in a cycle of pain and suffering. It prevents us from moving forward, reclaiming our sense of self-worth and dignity, and believing in the possibility of a brighter future.

One of the first steps in forgiving yourself is to practice self-compassion. This means treating yourself with the same kindness, understanding, and empathy you would extend to a dear friend or loved one struggling. It means recognizing that you are a flawed, imperfect human being who makes mistakes. Shame amounts to a break in the trust in your relationship with yourself. Your distrust of your spouse has spilled over into your relationship with yourself. Once again, start trusting yourself in your thinking, decisions, and actions. Just like everyone else, you deserve love and forgiveness, even in the face of pain and betrayal.

Part of trusting yourself again involves letting go of self-hatred and self-blame for what happened. The betrayer chose to cheat, not you. Accept that you could not control them at the time of the affair, and you do not control them now.

Self-compassion might involve talking to yourself in a gentle, nurturing way rather than engaging in harsh self-criticism or blame. It could mean engaging in activities that bring you joy, comfort, and relaxation, such as spending time in nature, practicing yoga or meditation, or pursuing a beloved hobby. It might also involve seeking out support from trusted friends, family members, or a therapist who can offer a listening ear and a compassionate perspective.

Another key aspect of self-forgiveness is learning to separate your partner's choices from your own worth and value as a person. It's essential to recognize that your partner's decision to cheat was not a reflection on you or your worthiness of love and respect. Your partner made a choice based on their own internal struggles, insecurities, or unmet needs - it was not a commentary on your value as a human being.

This can be a challenging idea to internalize, especially if you have a history of low self-esteem or codependency. Recognize that you do not have to be perfect. However, you can untangle your identity from your partner's actions and choices by consciously reminding yourself of your inherent worth and cultivating a strong sense of self-love and self-acceptance. For some of you who struggle with love addictions, this may seem an overwhelming task. Your identity is not based on your spouse's choices.

As you work on forgiving yourself, practicing self-care and setting healthy boundaries is important. This might involve taking time and space away from your partner to focus on your own healing and growth or setting clear limits around your emotional and physical availability. It could mean investing in your own interests, friendships, and goals rather than deriving your sense of self-worth solely from your relationship. For some of you, recognizing and acknowledging that you are a distinct individual with different interests and goals may be unsettling. Although the two of you formed a union, you don't have to lose yourself in the process.

Ultimately, forgiving yourself is about choosing to let go of the burden of shame, guilt, and self-blame you have been carrying. It's about recognizing that you are not responsible for your partner's choices and that you deserve to heal, grow, and thrive, regardless of what has happened in the past.

This process of self-forgiveness is not easy and will take time and practice to fully integrate into your life. The difficult part is being honest with yourself about what you need to forgive yourself for. There may be moments when old patterns of self-criticism or self-doubt resurface, and that's okay. What matters is that you continue to extend compassion and understanding to yourself, even in the face of setbacks or challenges.

Forgiving yourself is not about excusing or minimizing the pain of the betrayal. It's not about letting your partner off the hook or taking responsibility for their actions. Rather, it's about reclaiming your own sense of self-love, self-worth, and self-respect. It's about choosing to move forward with grace, resilience, and hope, even in the face of difficult circumstances.

By practicing self-forgiveness, you open yourself up to the possibility of a brighter, more fulfilling future - one in which you are able to love and accept yourself fully, regardless of what others may do or say. You remind yourself that you are worthy of love, respect, and happiness and that no one else's choices or actions can diminish your inherent value as a human being.

Moving past shame requires you to connect with others rather than hide from them. This means you need a support system of friends and family. Connecting with others may seem counterintuitive, but it will help lessen the noise in your head associated with shame and counter the negative self-talk that may be going on in your head.

## Reflection Questions:

1. In what ways have you been blaming or criticizing yourself in the aftermath of the affair? How can you practice self-compassion and kindness in these moments of self-judgment?

2. What beliefs or stories do you hold about your worth and value that may keep you stuck in feelings of shame or inadequacy? How can you begin to challenge and reframe these beliefs?

3. What self-care practices or boundaries do you need to put in place to prioritize your healing and well-being? How can you cultivate a stronger sense of self-love and self-acceptance?

4. Consider how you can retell the story of the affair from different perspectives. Consider one version where you are totally at fault, another where the blame is shared, and a third where the blame all falls on the betrayer. How did the story outcomes change? After retelling the story, drop the one where you are totally at fault since you do not have that much control.

5. What friends or family members can you spend time with that will accept you for who you are?

Forgiving yourself is a radical act of self-love and self-empowerment. By releasing the burden of shame and self-blame, you open yourself up to a future of greater peace, joy, and fulfillment. Trust in your resilience, lean on your support systems, and know that you are worthy of forgiveness, healing, and love, no matter the challenges you have faced.

# Chapter Twelve

# Preventing Future Affairs

"Once a woman has forgiven her man,
she must not reheat his sins for breakfast".
~Marlene Dietrich, "Forgiveness," Marlene
Dietrich's A B C, 1962

When Sophie and her husband, James, decided to rebuild their marriage after James's affair, they knew that forgiveness was only the first step. To truly heal and move forward, they would need to take a deep, honest look at the factors that had contributed to the breakdown of their relationship and make intentional changes to prevent future betrayals.

At first, this process felt overwhelming and even scary. Sophie and James had to confront painful truths about their communication styles, unmet needs, and how they had taken each other for granted. This included talking about how they drifted apart and differences in what each wanted in the bedroom. James grew up in a family where sex was not talked about, so having a frank discussion with Sophie was challenging for him.

They had to have difficult conversations about trust, boundaries, and accountability and commit to prioritizing their relationship in new and meaningful ways. Prior to the affair, there were few boundaries. Now, they had to talk about where James was, who he was with, being tested at the doctor's office regularly, and talking with Sophie about their finances.

If you are in a situation similar to Sophie and James's, it's essential to understand that preventing future affairs requires a proactive, intentional approach. It's not enough to simply forgive and move on—you must be willing to do the hard work to examine your relationship dynamics, address underlying issues, and make sustainable changes.

One of the first steps in preventing future affairs is to identify and address any contributing factors that may have led to the betrayal. This might involve exploring issues such as unresolved conflicts, mismatched expectations, or a lack of emotional and physical intimacy in the relationship.

It could also mean examining external stressors such as work demands, financial pressures, or family obligations that may have strained the relationship or created opportunities for temptation. By honestly and openly discussing these factors, you and your partner can begin to develop strategies for managing stress, communicating more effectively, and creating a more supportive and connected relationship dynamic.

Another key aspect of preventing future affairs is establishing clear boundaries and expectations around fidelity, transparency, and accountability. This might involve setting specific guidelines around opposite-sex friendships, social media use, or time spent apart from each other. Make what is and is not allowed clear. It could also mean establishing regular check-ins or allowing your spouse veto power over your social media contacts, creating a shared understanding of what constitutes a breach of trust in your relationship. It may also go so far as to ask for your spouse's input when hiring members of the opposite sex.

It's important to approach these conversations with a spirit of collaboration and mutual respect rather than from a place of suspicion or control.

The goal is not to police each other's behavior or create an atmosphere of fear and mistrust but rather to foster a sense of safety, security, and commitment to the relationship.

As you work to establish boundaries and expectations, it's also essential to prioritize building and maintaining a strong, intimate connection with your partner. This means making time for regular date nights, sharing new experiences and adventures together, and finding ways to express love, appreciation, and desire for each other daily.

It might also involve exploring new forms of physical and emotional intimacy, such as trying out new sexual techniques, engaging in vulnerable conversations about your hopes and fears, or expressing affection through small acts of kindness and generosity. By actively cultivating a sense of closeness and connection, you create a powerful buffer against the temptation of outside relationships or distractions.

Investing in personal growth and self-awareness is another important aspect of preventing future affairs. This means taking responsibility for your own healing, happiness, and fulfillment rather than relying solely on your partner to meet all of your needs.

It might involve individual therapy or counseling to work through past traumas, develop healthier coping strategies, or build stronger self-esteem and self-worth. It could also mean cultivating a rich and meaningful life outside of your relationship, with supportive friendships, hobbies, and personal goals that bring you joy and satisfaction.

By prioritizing your own growth and well-being, you become a more resilient and fulfilled individual and bring a greater sense of vitality, passion, and purpose to your relationship.

Ultimately, preventing future affairs requires a long-term commitment to the health and happiness of your relationship. It means being willing to have ongoing conversations about your needs, desires, and challenges and making a daily choice to prioritize your connection and intimacy with your partner.

This is not always an easy or straightforward process, and there may be moments of struggle, setback, or uncertainty along the way. However, by approaching this journey with patience, compassion, and a willingness to learn and grow, you and your partner can create a stronger, more resilient, and more deeply fulfilling relationship than ever before.

## Reflection Questions:

1. What factors or dynamics in your relationship may have contributed to the affair? How can you and your partner work together to address these issues and create a more supportive and connected relationship?

2. What boundaries or expectations must you establish to feel safe, respected, and valued in your relationship? How can you communicate these needs clearly and compassionately to your partner?

3. How can you prioritize your personal growth, healing, and self-awareness as you work to prevent future affairs? What support systems or resources do you need to cultivate a strong sense of self-love and self-worth?

Preventing future affairs is an ongoing, collaborative process that requires dedication, vulnerability, and a willingness to grow and change. By committing to this journey, you and your partner have the opportunity to not only heal from past betrayals but also to create a relationship that is more loving, trusting, and intimately connected than ever before. Trust in the process, lean on each other for support and know that a stronger, more beautiful relationship is possible with patience, understanding, and a shared commitment to your future.

# Chapter Thirteen

# Finding Meaning and Purpose

As Maria and her husband, Roberto, worked to rebuild their marriage after Roberto's infidelity, they found themselves grappling with deep questions about the meaning and purpose of their relationship. The affair had shattered their sense of trust and security, leaving them feeling lost, uncertain, and even hopeless at times. The meaning of marriage changed for each of them.

However, as they continued on their journey of healing and forgiveness, Maria and Roberto began to realize that the crisis of the affair could also be an opportunity for growth, learning, and transformation. It gave them a way to rewrite the story of their relationship. They started to explore what they truly valued in their relationship, what kind of future they wanted to create together, and how they could use their experiences to help others who were struggling with similar challenges.

If you find yourself in a situation like Maria and Roberto's, it's important to remember that healing from infidelity is not just about repairing the damage of the past - it's also about creating a new, more meaningful, and purposeful future together. By intentionally exploring your values, goals, and aspirations, you and your partner can begin to build a relationship that is not only stronger and more resilient but also more deeply aligned with your authentic selves and your highest purpose.

One way to begin this process is to take time to reflect on the lessons and insights you have gained from the experience of the affair. While the pain and betrayal of infidelity can be overwhelming, it can also be a powerful catalyst for personal growth and transformation.

You might ask yourself questions such as: What have I learned about myself, my partner, and our relationship through this experience? What have I learned about their needs and how to approach them? How has this crisis challenged me to grow, change, or evolve in ways that I might not have otherwise? What strengths, skills, or resources have I developed as a result of navigating this difficult journey?

By intentionally reflecting on these questions and sharing your insights with your partner, you can begin to reframe the affair experience as an opportunity for learning, healing, and growth. You can start to see the challenges you have faced not as a sign of failure or inadequacy but as a testament to your resilience, courage, and commitment to your relationship.

Another key aspect of finding meaning and purpose after infidelity is clarifying and recommitting to your shared values and vision for the future. This might involve having honest, vulnerable conversations about what truly matters to you as individuals and as a couple and what kind of life you want to create together moving forward.

You might explore questions such as: What are our deepest values and priorities in this relationship? Is our relationship about love, great sex, photo ops, having adventures, or making an impact? What kind of love, connection, and intimacy do we want to cultivate? What shared goals, dreams, or aspirations do we have for our future together? How can we align our daily actions, choices, and behaviors with these values and vision?

Few couples have sat down and seriously considered their priorities and goals. In tackling a tough topic like this, consider where you want your relationship to be in seven years. What kind of life do the two of you want to be having? Is it about a quiet life in the countryside or all-the-time activity in the bustling city?

These questions are important because they give you direction and motivation as you recover from what happened. You need a vision and direction; otherwise, the relationship is about being roommates with whom you settle.

By intentionally clarifying and recommitting to your shared values and vision, you create a powerful sense of meaning, direction, and purpose in your relationship. This gives you future direction rather than being defined by what happened. You remind yourselves of the deeper reasons why you chose to be together in the first place, and you create a roadmap for navigating the challenges and opportunities that lie ahead.

As you continue on this journey of finding meaning and purpose, it can also be incredibly healing and empowering to find ways to give back and make a positive difference in the lives of others. This might involve sharing your story of healing and forgiveness with other couples who are struggling with infidelity or volunteering your time and resources to support organizations that help individuals and families in crisis.

It could also mean becoming a mentor, coach, or counselor to others who are navigating similar challenges or using your experiences to inspire and encourage others to prioritize their own growth, healing, and transformation. By finding ways to turn your pain into purpose and your struggles into service, you deepen your sense of meaning and fulfillment and create a ripple effect of positive change in the world around you.

Ultimately, finding meaning and purpose after infidelity is about choosing to see the experience as a catalyst for growth, learning, and transformation. It's about intentionally creating a future that is not defined by the wounds of the past but rather by the strength, resilience, and love that you have cultivated through the journey of healing.

This is not always an easy or straightforward process, and there may be moments of doubt, fear, or uncertainty along the way. However, by approaching this journey with curiosity, compassion, and a willingness to learn and grow, you and your partner can discover a deeper, richer, and more fulfilling meaning and purpose than ever before.

## Re-Labeling

The next stage in cleaning your head after forgiveness involves re-labeling. It is important that you forgive before starting Re-Labeling.

Re-labeling or re-framing is a powerful tool for changing your views of the affair, the people involved, and the events. However, it is crucial to engage in re-labeling only after you have forgiven. Engaging in re-labeling prior to forgiving will lead to confusion and make cleaning out your head more difficult.

Re-labeling involves taking the incidents surrounding the affair and changing the meaning you associate with them. Some aspects you can change. If you can change them, such as changing your surroundings, etc. do it. For those that cannot be changed, the answer is re-labeling.

In re-labeling, you will first identify the incidents needing re-labeling. Once you have the list, you can begin the process. Take each incident and explore other 'possible' meanings. Rather than taking each incident as a personal attack, which will leave you feeling defensive, start looking at the possibility that there may be another meaning or even several meanings.

It will take mental flexibility to 're-label'. Many people find it challenging to even consider the possibility that the event has other meanings than what they have already come up with. When you start the process, your thinking will become more 'fluid' regarding the affair. Re-labeling does not change what happened; it changes the meanings you associate with those events.

If you are like most people, you will need to write down the incident, along with its meaning. You will need to brainstorm other possible meanings and write them down as well. Then, you can put an "X" on the old meaning and allow your mind to see the possibility of other meanings.

Once your mind sees the new meaning in black and white, it helps make the 'new' mental connection. After a cognitive link between the event and meaning is made, then you can start making new emotional changes. The emotional changes follow changes in thinking. When you change your thinking, your emotions will change as well. At first, the change will seem artificial. Over time, the new meaning will become more natural.

## Reflection Questions:

1. What lessons, insights, or strengths have you gained from the experience of healing from infidelity? How can you use these experiences to grow, learn, and evolve as individuals and as a couple?

2. What are your deepest values, priorities, and aspirations for your relationship? How can you align your actions, choices, and behaviors with these values and vision on a daily basis?

3. How can you use your experiences to make a positive difference in the lives of others? How can you find purpose and fulfillment by turning your pain into service and your struggles into support for others?

Finding meaning and purpose after infidelity is a courageous and transformative act of love. By choosing to see this experience as an opportunity for growth, learning, and service, you open yourself up to a future that is not only healed from the wounds of the past but also deeply aligned with your authentic self and your highest purpose. Trust in the journey, lean on each other for support, and know that a life of profound meaning and fulfillment is possible with patience, compassion, and a willingness to grow and learn.

# Chapter Fourteen

# Regret, Remorse and Repentance

"Repentance means you change your mind so deeply that it changes you." Bruce Wilkinson

In the process of healing from infidelity, the concept of forgiveness is often closely intertwined with the ideas of regret, remorse, and repentance expressed by the betrayer. These three terms, collectively referred to as the "3Rs," describe the betrayer's expression of sorrow for their actions. While forgiveness is about letting go of negative emotions for your own peace of mind and opening up the possibility of reconciliation, the 3Rs are about the offender taking steps to reconcile the marriage relationship. This chapter explores the nuances of the 3Rs and their relationship to forgiveness, providing guidance on navigating the complex emotions and expectations that arise when a betrayer seeks forgiveness.

Eve and Tom had been working on moving past the pain of the affair. Eve has been reluctant to forgive for a long time since Tom has not asked for forgiveness. She believed he was not accepting responsibility for his actions or showing remorse. After a while, Tom admitted to doing wrong and asked her to forgive him.

Eve had wanted to hear those words for so long. Now that she heard them, something still didn't feel right about it. Although he asked for forgiveness, she wasn't sure if this was enough. Eve was caught up in what I call the 3Rs.

An area associated with forgiveness is "Regret, Remorse, and Repentance." These three terms describe when the betrayer expresses sorrow for what they have done. I often use the three terms interchangeably, so I call them the 3Rs.

The betrayer may approach you with the 3Rs and ask you for forgiveness as part of expressing their sorrow. Since this request for forgiveness is so closely intertwined with forgiveness, it is often termed 'forgiveness' as well.

Confusing the 3Rs with forgiveness can trip you up. Forgiveness is letting go of things for your own peace of mind and opening up the possibility of reconciliation. The 3Rs are about the offender taking steps to reconcile your marriage relationship.

When the cheater admits what they are doing and expresses sorrow or regret with the intention of turning from what they did, it would be one of the 3Rs. When the cheater is truly repentant, they'll admit what they did, acknowledge it was wrong, validate how it impacted you, ask for forgiveness, and take steps to correct the damage they contributed to. On top of that, they do it all without defensiveness!

When all the cheater does is admit what they did, it's often a half-hearted repentance. Just admitting what happened can occur when they finally face the facts about the affair.

It sounds complicated, yet each piece of a full 3R statement is important.

1. Admit what happened
2. Acknowledge that what they did was 'wrong'
3. Validate how it impacted you
4. Ask forgiveness

5. Take steps to correct the damage

When they seriously mean business, you will see changes in their behavior and their thinking. When you only see changes in one area, they are going through the motions of the 3Rs without being fully invested in change.

When they approach you with the 3Rs, it puts you on the spot. That's okay. Just because they ask for it does not mean that you have to forgive them. You may not be ready for that yet. That does not make you a bad person or an uncaring person.

Since a 3R situation often involves high emotions, there is a temptation to forgive to reduce the tension. In such cases, the forgiveness was premature. Emotional tension is often a good thing, as the discomfort it brings often drives people to make changes. That tension is a powerful motivator.

**Some general guidelines for genuine repentance are:**

1. The offender must take full and total responsibility for the offense

2. The offender must demonstrate appropriate remorse for the offense and the extent of damage done to the victim

3. Offenders must establish adequate boundaries that demonstrate proper respect for the victim and provide future safety for the victim

4. Offenders must actively change behavior patterns that led to the offense


# Reflection Questions:

1. How can you distinguish between genuine repentance (3Rs) and a manipulative attempt to gain forgiveness without true change?

2. What steps can you take to ensure that you are not pressured into premature forgiveness when your partner expresses the 3Rs?

3. How can you clearly communicate your needs and expectations to your partner when they express regret, remorse, or repentance?

4. How can you balance the desire for reconciliation with the need for your partner to demonstrate consistent, long-term changes in behavior and thinking?

5. What support systems or resources can you rely on to help you navigate the complex emotions and challenges that arise when your partner expresses the 3Rs?

Remember, the 3Rs can be a powerful step towards healing and reconciliation, but only when they are genuine, consistent, and accompanied by lasting changes in behavior and thinking. By understanding the nuances of regret, remorse, and repentance and by prioritizing your own emotional well-being and safety, you can navigate this challenging aspect of the forgiveness process with wisdom, compassion, and strength.

# Part IV: Navigating Complex Situations

Restore The Family Press

---

# Chapter Fifteen

# The Role of Couples Therapy in Healing

As we've explored the process of forgiveness and healing after infidelity, it's important to acknowledge that every couple's journey is unique. Some situations may present additional challenges or complexities that require special consideration and guidance.

In this part of the book, we'll look into three key areas that can significantly impact the forgiveness process: the role of couples therapy, cultural and religious considerations, and the presence of abuse or unhealthy power dynamics in the relationship.

Through exploring these topics, we aim to provide a more nuanced and comprehensive understanding of the diverse factors that can shape a couple's experience of infidelity and their path to healing. Whether you're considering seeking professional help, grappling with cultural or religious influences, or dealing with a history of abuse, the insights and strategies in these chapters will offer valuable guidance and support.

As we navigate these complex situations together, remember that healing is possible even in the face of great challenges. By approaching these issues with openness, compassion, and a commitment to your well-being, you can continue moving forward on your journey of forgiveness and growth.

When Ethan and Olivia decided to seek couples therapy after Ethan's affair, they were both nervous and unsure about what to expect. They had been trying to work through the fallout of the infidelity on their own but kept getting stuck in cycles of blame, defensiveness, and hurt. They knew they needed help but were afraid of opening up to a stranger about their most painful and private struggles.

As they began their therapy journey, however, Ethan and Olivia quickly discovered the value of having a safe, neutral space to process their emotions, communicate their needs, and develop new ways of talking with each other and solving their differences. With their therapist's guidance and support, they could navigate difficult conversations, uncover deeper issues and patterns, and begin to rebuild trust and intimacy in their relationship.

Ethan struggled to identify and express what he was feeling. With the help of the therapy, he was finally able to do so, and then Olivia finally understood where he was coming from along with the struggles he went through.

If you and your partner are considering couples therapy as part of your healing process after infidelity, it's important to understand the role that therapy can play in your journey. While therapy is not a magic solution or a guarantee of success, it can be a powerful tool for facilitating communication, insight, and change.

One of the primary benefits of couples therapy is that it provides a structured, supportive environment for working through complex emotions and experiences related to infidelity. In the aftermath of an affair, it's common for couples to struggle with intense feelings of anger, betrayal, guilt, shame, and fear. These emotions can make it difficult to communicate effectively, listen empathetically, or maintain a sense of safety and trust in the relationship.

A skilled and experienced therapist can help couples navigate these challenging emotions in a healthy, productive, and nonjudgmental way. They can provide tools and strategies for expressing feelings assertively, listening actively, and handling differences without defensive reactions and arguing. They can also help couples identify and challenge unhelpful thought patterns, assumptions, and behaviors that may perpetuate conflict or disconnection.

Another key role of couples therapy is to help partners identify and address deeper issues and patterns that may have contributed to the infidelity or that may be hindering the healing process. Often, affairs do not occur in a vacuum but are symptomatic of longer-standing problems in the relationship, such as unmet emotional needs, communication breakdowns, or unresolved conflicts.

In therapy, couples can explore these underlying issues in a safe and structured way, with the guidance of a neutral third party. They can gain new insights into their own and each other's perspectives, needs, and behaviors and develop a shared understanding of the work that needs to be done to heal and strengthen their relationship.

Couples therapy can also be a valuable resource for developing new skills and strategies for rebuilding trust, intimacy, and connection after infidelity. Therapists can teach couples evidence-based techniques for improving communication, such as active listening, "I" statements, and conflict resolution skills. They can also guide couples through exercises and experiences designed to promote empathy, vulnerability, and bonding, such as emotional check-ins, gratitude practices, or shared adventures and hobbies.

In addition to these benefits, couples therapy can also provide account-ability, motivation, and support for the hard work of healing and growth. Attending regular therapy sessions can help couples prioritize their relationship and stay committed to the forgiveness process, even when it feels challenging or discouraging. It can also provide a sense of hope, validation, and normalization as couples realize that they are not alone in their struggles and that growth and healing are possible.

When seeking couples therapy, it's important to find a therapist who is trained and experienced in working with couples and who has specific expertise in infidelity and affair recovery. Look for a non-judgmental, empathetic, and direct therapist who creates a safe and supportive environment for both partners to share and explore.

It's also important to approach therapy with realistic expectations and a willingness to engage fully in the process. Therapy is not a quick fix or a passive experience but rather a collaborative and active journey that requires both partners' commitment, courage, and vulnerability.

Ultimately, couples therapy's role in healing from infidelity is to provide a safe, supportive, and structured space for couples to process their experiences, learn new skills, and create positive change in their relationship. By working with a skilled therapist and committing fully to the process, couples can deepen their understanding of themselves and each other, heal from the wounds of betrayal, and build a stronger, more resilient bond moving forward.

## Reflection Questions:

1. What hopes, fears, or expectations do you have about engaging in couples therapy? How can you discuss these with your partner and/or therapist?

2. What specific issues or challenges in your relationship do you hope to address in therapy? How can you communicate these goals clearly and collaboratively with your partner and therapist?

3. What qualities or characteristics are most important to you in a couples therapist? How can you and your partner work together to find a therapist who is a good fit for your needs and goals?

Engaging in couples therapy after infidelity is a brave and powerful step towards healing, growth, and renewed connection. By embracing the process with openness, vulnerability, and commitment, you and your partner can unlock new levels of understanding, empathy, and intimacy and create a stronger, wiser, and more loving relationship.

# Chapter Sixteen

# Forgiveness and Healing Across Cultures

When Priya and Raj, a Hindu couple from India, faced the aftermath of Raj's infidelity, they found themselves grappling not only with the personal and relational fallout but also with the cultural and religious expectations surrounding marriage, loyalty, and forgiveness. Priya felt a deep sense of shame and failure, believing that she had somehow fallen short of her duties as a wife and that she would be judged harshly by her community if they knew of Raj's betrayal.

Similarly, when Fatima and Hassan, a Muslim couple from Lebanon, confronted Hassan's affair, they had to navigate the complex interplay of their faith, their cultural values, and their personal beliefs about love, commitment, and reconciliation. Fatima struggled with the idea of forgiveness, wondering if it was truly possible or permissible within the context of their religious and cultural traditions.

For couples like Priya and Raj and Fatima and Hassan, the journey of healing and forgiveness after infidelity is shaped not only by their individual experiences and emotions but also by the larger cultural and religious frameworks that inform their identities, relationships, and worldviews. While the pain of betrayal is universal, the way that couples make meaning of and respond to infidelity can vary widely based on their cultural background, religious beliefs, and social context. Not only is infidelity looked at differently, but so is forgiveness. What forgiveness means and how it is approached varies with cultures.

In some cultures, for example, infidelity may be seen as a deeply shameful and unforgivable act, one that brings dishonor to the entire family or community. In these contexts, couples may face intense pressure to keep the affair secret, to preserve public appearances, or to seek quick and decisive solutions, such as separation or divorce, rather than work through the issues. In these situations, the shame makes talking about the affair and working through it challenging. Those involved may consider one conversation about it enough.

In other cultures, there may be strong religious or moral injunctions against infidelity, with clear teachings and expectations around fidelity, repentance, and forgiveness. Couples in these contexts may wrestle with questions of sin, redemption, and spiritual accountability and may look to religious leaders or teachings for guidance and support.

Still, other cultures may have more flexible or permissive attitudes towards infidelity, viewing it as a relatively common or understandable transgression or as a private matter between partners. Couples in these contexts may have more latitude in navigating the healing process on their own terms but may also face less social support or validation for their experiences.

Regardless of the specific cultural or religious context, it's important for couples dealing with infidelity to recognize and honor the ways that their background and beliefs shape their experiences and choices. There are some common struggles and helps. This may involve:

  1. Examining cultural and religious messages: Taking time to reflect on the explicit and implicit messages they have received about

relationships, loyalty, forgiveness, and betrayal, and how these messages impact their current situation. They still have the choice of how to apply those messages to their marriage.

2. Seeking culturally sensitive support: Find a therapist, counselor, or support group that is knowledgeable and respectful of their cultural and religious background and can help them navigate the intersection of their personal and cultural identities. This is especially true with couples who each have distinctly different cultural backgrounds when it comes to infidelity and forgiveness.

3. Balancing personal and cultural needs: Working to find a path that honors their needs and desires while respecting and incorporating the cultural and religious values important to them and their community. This includes what is expected of the man and the woman and the positions each has.

4. Challenging stereotypes and assumptions: Being willing to question and resist cultural or religious stereotypes or expectations that may be limiting or harmful, such as the idea that forgiveness is always required, that infidelity is always unforgivable, or that beatings are an acceptable way of dealing with such matters.

5. Embracing cultural strengths and resources: Drawing upon the unique strengths, traditions, and resources of their cultural and religious heritage, such as practices of prayer, meditation, ritual, or community support, to aid in their healing and growth.

Ultimately, the path of forgiveness and healing after infidelity is a deeply personal and intimate journey, one that is shaped by each couple's unique history, context, and identity. By embracing the diversity of their experiences and backgrounds and by finding ways to honor and integrate their cultural and religious beliefs into their healing process, couples from all walks of life can find a way to navigate the pain of betrayal and emerge stronger, wiser, and more loving on the other side.

## Reflection Questions:

1. In what ways have your cultural, religious, or family background shaped your beliefs and expectations about relationships, fidelity, and forgiveness? How are these beliefs impacting your current situation?

2. What cultural or religious resources, practices, or traditions can you draw upon to support your healing and growth in the aftermath of infidelity? How can you incorporate these into your journey of forgiveness?

3. What stereotypes, assumptions, or expectations from your culture or religion may be limiting or harmful as you navigate the infidelity and healing process? How can you challenge or resist these messages in a way that honors your own needs and values?

Your cultural and religious background is integral to who you are and how you make meaning of your experiences. By embracing the diversity and complexity of your identity and by finding ways to honor and integrate your cultural and spiritual beliefs into your healing process, you can chart a path towards forgiveness and transformation that is uniquely and authentically your own.

# Chapter Seventeen

# Forgiveness, Abuse, and Power Dynamics

"Father, forgive them, for they don't know what they are doing."~ Luke 23:34

When Emily discovered her partner Sarah's affair, she was devastated. However, as she processed her emotions and reflected on their relationship, she began to recognize patterns of emotional abuse and manipulation that had been present long before the infidelity. Sarah would frequently criticize and belittle Emily, control her social interactions, and threaten to leave her if she didn't comply with her demands. The affair, Emily realized, was just another way for Sarah to exert power and control over their relationship. Sarah was exploiting Emily's fears of abandonment. Those fears kept her paralyzed and stuck in the relationship.

For couples like Emily and Sarah, the issue of infidelity is often intertwined with larger patterns of abuse, control, and unhealthy power dynamics. In these situations, the betrayal of trust and the violation of boundaries that come with infidelity can be particularly traumatic and destabilizing, compounding the pre-existing harm and fear within the relationship.

It's important to recognize that reconciliation is not always safe, appropriate, or possible in relationships where abuse or exploitation is present. While forgiveness can be a powerful tool for personal healing and liberation, it should never come at the cost of one's physical, emotional, or psychological safety and well-being. If there is a safety issue, your safety is the priority.

In relationships where there is a history of abuse or unhealthy power dynamics, it's crucial to prioritize safety and empowerment above all else. This may involve:

1. Recognizing signs of abuse: Learning to identify the signs and patterns of emotional, physical, financial, or sexual abuse, such as controlling behaviors, isolation, threats, or violence.

2. Seeking support and resources: Reaching out to trusted friends, family members, therapists, or domestic violence hotlines for support, guidance, and practical assistance in creating a safety plan and accessing resources. In dealing with such situations, you need a support network.

3. Setting firm boundaries: Communicating one's needs, limits, and expectations and enforcing consequences for any violations or breaches of trust.

4. Prioritizing safety: Focusing on one's own healing, growth, and independence and building a strong sense of self-worth and self-advocacy. Healing can only occur when each party feels safe.

5. Considering separation or ending the relationship: In situations where abuse is severe, chronic, or unresponsive to intervention, it may be necessary to consider separating from or ending the

relationship to ensure one's safety and well-being.

It's important to note that leaving an abusive relationship can be a difficult and dangerous process and should be done with careful planning and support. Seeking the guidance of a trained domestic violence advocate or therapist can be invaluable in navigating this challenging terrain.

For individuals who have experienced abuse and infidelity in their relationships, the journey of healing and forgiveness is more complex and layered. It may involve not only processing the pain and betrayal of the infidelity but also grappling with the trauma and fear of the abuse and the difficult decisions around whether to stay or leave the relationship. The formation of trauma bonds often keeps them locked into difficult situations.

In these situations, it's important to approach forgiveness as a deeply personal and individual choice - one that is grounded in self-love, self-protection, and self-determination. Forgiveness does not mean forgetting the abuse, minimizing its impact, or absolving the abuser of responsibility. Rather, it means making a conscious decision to release the hold that the pain and trauma have over one's life and to reclaim one's power, agency, and worth. It involves breaking the trauma bonds that kept them locked into the relationship.

This kind of forgiveness may or may not involve reconciliation with the abuser. They can be forgiven, yet the relationship may not be safe to continue. In some cases, it may be possible to rebuild a relationship if the abuser takes full responsibility for their actions, seeks professional help, and demonstrates sustained change over time. However, in many cases, the most loving and empowering choice may be to forgive from a distance and to focus on creating a new life of safety, healing, and wholeness.

Ultimately, the journey of forgiveness and healing in the context of abuse and infidelity is a courageous and transformative act of self-love and self-reclamation. By prioritizing one's safety, dignity, and well-being and by seeking the support and resources needed to navigate this difficult terrain, individuals can find a way to break free from the cycles of betrayal and harm and create a future of greater peace, power, and possibility.

## Reflection Questions:

1. If you have experienced abuse or unhealthy power dynamics in your relationship, what steps can you take to prioritize your safety and well-being? What support or resources do you need to create a plan for healing and empowerment?

2. How can you distinguish between the pain and betrayal of infidelity and the larger patterns of abuse or control in your relationship? What insights or revelations have you had about the dynamics of power and trust in your relationship?

3. What would forgiveness look and feel like for you in the context of abuse and infidelity? What boundaries, actions, or changes would you need to see in order to feel safe, respected, and empowered in your relationship moving forward?

Your safety and well-being are always the top priority. If you are in an abusive relationship, know that you are not alone and that there is help and support available. By reaching out for guidance, setting clear boundaries, and focusing on your healing and empowerment, you can break free from the cycles of betrayal and harm and create a future of greater peace, strength, and possibility.

# Part V: Sustaining Healing and Growth

Restore The Family Press

# Chapter Eighteen

# Maintaining Progress and Preventing Relapse

The journey of forgiveness and healing after infidelity is not a one-time event but an ongoing process that requires commitment, patience, and self-awareness. As you move forward on this path, it's essential to have strategies in place to maintain your progress, prevent setbacks, and continue cultivating a strong, resilient relationship. You may also have some questions. One question concerns how many times you will need to forgive the offender. When Jesus was presented with this question, He answered, "I say not unto thee, Until seven times: but Until seventy times seven." That answer shows that there are times when forgiveness requires significant effort.

In this final part of the book, we'll focus on two key aspects of long-term healing and growth: maintaining progress, preventing relapse, and accessing additional resources and support.

Through exploring these topics, we aim to equip you with the tools and knowledge needed to sustain the positive changes you've made and continue building a relationship that is grounded in trust, intimacy, and mutual understanding.

Whether you're looking for practical tips to keep your healing on track, seeking guidance on how to handle potential triggers or challenges, or wanting to expand your support system, the insights and strategies in these chapters will provide a roadmap for ongoing success.

When Liam and Sophia first began their journey of healing and forgiveness after Liam's affair, they were fully committed to doing the hard work of trying new ways of handling conflicts and improving how they talked to each other (this included changing their tone of voice and no longer interrupting each other) and rekindling intimacy. They attended couples therapy, read self-help books, and had countless deep conversations about their hopes, fears, and desires for the future. It took Liam a while to open up his heart to Sophia, and things seemed to be getting better for a while - they felt closer, more connected, and more optimistic about their relationship.

However, as time passed and the initial intensity of the healing process faded, Liam and Sophia began to slip back into old patterns of behavior. They stopped prioritizing their couple time, and phones received more attention than each other. They let resentments and misunderstandings build up and eventually found themselves feeling distant, disconnected, and vulnerable to new temptations and betrayals.

Liam and Sophia's experience is not uncommon. Many couples who have worked hard to heal and forgive after infidelity find that maintaining progress and preventing relapse over the long term can be just as challenging as the initial stages of recovery. Just as with any major life change or transformation, sustaining the gains made in therapy and ensuring ongoing growth and connection requires intentional effort, commitment, and strategies for success.

Some key strategies for maintaining progress and preventing relapse after infidelity include:

1. Continue to prioritize the relationship: Setting aside regular time for date nights, check-ins, and intimate conversations and treating the relationship as a top priority in terms of time, energy, and attention. Put down your phone and make your spouse the main focus of your attention. Aim to spend at least 20 minutes a day talking with each other. If you have not made much eye contact during that time, start doing so.

2. Practice effective communication: Using "I" statements, active listening, and conflict resolution skills to address issues and misunderstandings before they escalate and to ensure that both partners feel heard, validated, and respected.

3. Maintain accountability and transparency: Continue to be open and honest about one's thoughts, feelings, and actions and follow through on commitments to fidelity, honesty, and integrity. Make it a point to listen to understand rather than to formulate your defense.

4. Nurture individual growth and self-care: Encourage each partner to pursue their interests, friendships, and self-care practices and bring their best selves to the relationship. Be willing to do what your spouse enjoys.

5. Address underlying issues and triggers: Continue to work on any underlying personal or relational issues that may have contributed to the infidelity, such as unresolved trauma, attachment wounds, or communication breakdowns. You may also want to explore any family history of affairs and the patterns that they brought.

6. Seek ongoing support and resources: Start praying together, engage in booster sessions with a therapist, attend workshops or retreats, or join a support group for couples in recovery from infidelity.

7. Be proactive about potential warning signs: Pay attention to any red flags or warning signs of disconnection, such as decreased intimacy, increased secrecy, or a resurgence of old coping patterns, and address them quickly and directly.

Another important aspect of preventing relapse is having a clear and specific plan for how to handle any future temptations, boundary crossings, or lapses in judgment. This might include:

- Having a written contract or agreement about what constitutes infidelity or a breach of trust in the relationship and what the consequences and steps for repair would be.

- Identifying and avoiding any high-risk situations, people, or environments that could trigger old patterns or temptations.

- Having a support system of trusted friends, family members, or professionals who can provide accountability, guidance, and encouragement in moments of weakness or stress.

- Developing a repertoire of healthy coping strategies and self-soothing techniques for managing difficult emotions, stress, or triggers.

Ultimately, maintaining progress and preventing relapse after infidelity is an ongoing, lifelong process - one that requires patience, perseverance, and a deep commitment to growth and healing. It's not about achieving perfection or never making mistakes but rather about having the tools, strategies, and support systems in place to navigate the inevitable challenges and setbacks that arise and continue moving forward with love, trust, and resilience.

By prioritizing the relationship, practicing effective communication and self-care, addressing underlying issues and triggers, and being proactive about potential warning signs, couples can build a strong foundation for lasting recovery and create a relationship that is even stronger, more intimate, and more fulfilling than before the betrayal.

## Reflection Questions:

1. What strategies or practices have been most helpful for you in maintaining progress and connection in your relationship after infidelity? How can you continue to prioritize and implement these in your daily life?

2. What potential warning signs or triggers for relapse are you most concerned about in your own relationship? How can you and your partner work together to address these proactively and create a plan for prevention and repair?

3. What personal growth edges or self-care practices do you need to focus on to bring your best self to your relationship and support long-term healing and recovery? How can you make space for these in your daily routine and enlist support from your partner or others?

Remember, healing and forgiveness after infidelity are not a one-time event but an ongoing journey of growth, learning, and recommitment. By staying intentional, proactive, and compassionate with yourself and your partner and by reaching out for support and resources when needed, you can continue to deepen your connection, strengthen your resilience, and create a love that lasts a lifetime.

# Chapter Nineteen

# Resources and References

Throughout this book, we've explored the complex and challenging journey of healing and forgiveness after infidelity. We've discussed the importance of understanding what forgiveness is and is not, the process of letting go and rebuilding trust, the role of self-forgiveness and self-care, and strategies for maintaining progress and preventing relapse over the long term.

While this book provides a comprehensive foundation for the work of healing and recovery, it's important to remember that every individual and couple's journey is unique and may require additional support, guidance, and resources along the way. Below, you'll find a list of recommended books, websites, support groups, and therapist directories to help you continue learning, growing, and healing beyond the pages of this book.

**Recommended Books:**

1. "Not Just Friends: Rebuilding Trust and Recovering Your Sanity After Infidelity" by Shirley P. Glass

2. "Healing the Shame that Binds You" by John Bradshaw

3. "How Can I Forgive You? The Courage to Forgive, the Freedom Not To" by Janis A. Spring

4. "Out of the Shadows: Understanding Sexual Addiction" by Patrick Carnes

## Websites and Online Resources:

1. SurviveYourPartnersAffair.com - An online resource for couples coping with infidelity, offering articles, Q&A,

2. EmotionalAffair.org - An online community offering support, advice, and resources for individuals and couples dealing with infidelity.

3. AffairRecovery.com - Offers online courses, workshops, and resources for individuals and couples healing from infidelity.

4. InfidelityHelpGroup.com - Provides articles, resources, and a directory of therapists and support groups for those impacted by infidelity.

5. BeyondAffairs.com - Offers personal coaching, online courses, and resources for individuals and couples recovering from infidelity.

## Support Groups:

1. Infidelity Survivors Anonymous (ISA) - A 12-step program for individuals healing from the impact of a partner's infidelity.

2. Codependents of Sex Addicts (COSA) - A 12-step program for individuals impacted by a partner's compulsive sexual behavior or sex addiction.

3. Celebrating Men, Satisfying Women (CMSW) - Offers support groups and workshops for individuals and couples dealing with infidelity or sex addiction.

4. Betrayed Wives Club - An online support group and community for women healing from a partner's infidelity.

5. Infidelity Support Group - A directory of in-person and online support groups for individuals and couples coping with infidelity.

Remember, seeking additional support and resources is a sign of strength and commitment to your healing and growth. Whether you choose to explore one of these recommended resources or find your path to continued learning and support, know that you are not alone and that there is always hope for healing, renewal, and transformation after the pain of infidelity.

The journey of forgiveness and recovery is deeply personal and sacred—one that requires courage, vulnerability, and a willingness to face the unknown. By embracing the full range of your experiences and emotions, seeking out the support and guidance you need, and staying true to your path of healing and growth, you can emerge from this challenge stronger, wiser, and more deeply connected to yourself, your partner, and your highest purpose.

May this book and these additional resources be a source of hope, inspiration, and practical guidance as you navigate the uncharted territories of your own heart and relationship. May you always remember that no matter how lost or broken you may feel, you have the power to forgive, heal, and create a love that endures.

# Chapter Twenty

# The Journey Forward

Throughout this book, we have explored the challenging, transformative journey of healing and forgiveness after infidelity. We have walked alongside couples like Lena and Eric, Sophie and Liam, and Maria and Roberto, witnessing their struggles, their breakthroughs, and their unwavering commitment to love, growth, and healing.

Along the way, we have discovered that forgiveness is not a single act or decision but rather an ongoing process of letting go, shifting perspectives, choosing to create a new future together, and relabeling what happened. We have learned that rebuilding trust requires patience, vulnerability, and a willingness to confront hard truths and make meaningful changes. We have seen that finding meaning and purpose in the aftermath of betrayal is possible and can be a catalyst for profound personal and relational transformation.

As you reflect on your own journey of healing and forgiveness, it's important to remember that there is no one-size-fits-all path or timeline for this process. Each individual, each couple, and each situation is unique, with its own challenges, complexities, and opportunities for growth.

Some couples may find that they are able to move through the stages of healing relatively quickly, while others may need more time, support, and guidance along the way. Some individuals may discover that forgiveness comes easily and naturally to them, while others may struggle with intense feelings of anger, betrayal, and mistrust for months or even years.

Regardless of where you find yourself on this journey, what matters most is your commitment to your own healing, growth, and well-being. This means being patient and compassionate with yourself, honoring your needs and boundaries, and seeking the support and resources you need to navigate this challenging terrain.

It also means being willing to lean into the discomfort and uncertainty of the journey, trusting that even the most painful experiences can be opportunities for learning, transformation, and renewed intimacy and connection. By embracing the full range of your emotions, communicating openly and honestly with your partner, and staying true to your deepest values and aspirations, you can begin to create a future that is not defined by the wounds of the past but rather by the strength, resilience, and love that you have cultivated along the way.

As you progress on this journey, remember that forgiveness and healing are not destinations to be reached but ongoing practices to be cultivated and nurtured over time. There will be moments of progress and celebration, as well as moments of setbacks and struggle. There will be days when you feel a deep sense of connection, trust, and intimacy with your partner and days when old wounds and doubts resurface.

In these moments, it's essential to return to the principles and practices that have guided you thus far - to choose love over fear, compassion over judgment, and growth over stagnation. It's also important to surround yourself with a supportive community of friends, family, and professionals who can offer guidance, encouragement, and accountability along the way.

Remember, the journey of healing and forgiveness is not a solo venture but a collaborative process that requires the support, love, and commitment of many. By reaching out for help when you need it, sharing your story with others who can relate and understand, and offering your own wisdom and compassion to those who are struggling, you become part of a larger community of healing and hope.

Ultimately, the journey of forgiveness and healing after infidelity is a testament to the incredible resilience, courage, and capacity for love within us. It reminds us that even in the face of the deepest pain and betrayal, we have the power to choose a different story, a different future, and a different way of being in the world.

As you continue on this path, trust in your strength, wisdom, and ability to love. If you don't have enough, ask for more. This may entail utilizing spiritual resources. Embrace the fullness of your journey, with all its joys and sorrows, challenges and triumphs. And know that with each step you take, you are healing your heart and relationship and contributing to a larger story of hope, healing, and transformation in the world.

The journey forward may not always be easy, but it is always worth it. May you find the courage, compassion, and commitment to keep going, one day at a time, one moment at a time, one breath at a time. And may you discover, in the end, that the path of forgiveness and healing is not only a journey back to love but also a journey forward to a life of greater meaning, purpose, and fulfillment than you ever thought possible.

As you embark on this transformative journey of forgiveness and healing, remember that you are not alone. Countless others have walked this path before you, facing the same fears, doubts, and challenges and emerging stronger, wiser, and more compassionate on the other side. Trust in the resilience of the human spirit, the power of love, and the potential for growth that lies within every challenge. Embrace the full spectrum of your experiences, both the joys and the sorrows, knowing that each step brings you closer to a future of greater peace, purpose, and connection. Above all, hold fast to the hope that lies at the heart of forgiveness - the hope of a new beginning, a renewed relationship, and a love that endures. In this hope, we find the courage to let go, heal, and build the life and love we truly deserve.

# About The Author

As a teenager, I experienced the devastation caused by infidelity first-hand when my family went through a parental affair. Navigating through the aftermath, which involved children's protective services, domestic abuse, legal fights, and emotional upheaval, left me feeling helpless and alone.

Determined to learn from these experiences, I became a Licensed Professional Counselor (LPC) and Licensed Chemical Dependency Counselor (LCDC). For over 40 years, I have helped thousands of families across various settings, applying an approach founded on proven Biblical principles and neuropsychology discoveries.

As an early pioneer in online counseling, I have been helping people through articles, e-books, and telephone sessions since 1999. My work has been featured on Wall Street Journal Radio, the Larry Elder Show, and numerous other media.

Married since 1985, my wife Peggy and I have been blessed with three incredible sons. We have navigated the challenges and temptations in our own marriage, and I am committed to helping others overcome the pain of affairs and rebuild their relationships.

As a licensed professional counselor with over 45 years of experience in the counseling field in many settings, I can offer expertise from many angles. I have worked in hospitals, drug rehabs, foster homes, outpatient clinics, biofeedback labs, schools, churches, and homeless shelters.

My work has included dealing with Parent Alienation Syndrome and expert witness work regarding family and mental health matters, including addictions and recovering from them. I have helped my clients directly through articles, blog posts, and media appearances on the Wall Street Journal radio program.

In 2010, I was selected for inclusion in the **"Counseling Courier's Marriage Counselor Hall of Fame"** as one of the top 15 counselors. You can also find my articles on Medium.com @RestoreTheFamily.

**My specialty** is working with couples recovering from affairs. My experiences include extensive dealing with these issues from a Christian counseling perspective. I am also a Certified Mental Health & Nutrition Clinical Specialist (CMNCS) and Farm Response Certified. You may contact me via email at jeff@restorethefamily.com.

Follow me on Medium @RestoreTheFamily.

Receive my daily newsletter at www.SurviveYourPartnersAffair.com

# The Affair Recovery Workhop

## Transform Your Marriage

Are you ready to embark on a transformative journey to heal your marriage and rediscover the love, trust, and intimacy you once shared? The Affair Recovery Workshop, created by renowned relationship expert Jeffrey D. Murrah, LPC, LCDC, is your essential companion to this book, offering a unique and comprehensive approach to navigating the complex emotions and challenges that follow infidelity. With a proven track record of success and a personalized approach tailored to your needs, this workshop provides you with the in-depth guidance, interactive experience, and practical tools necessary to rebuild a stronger, more resilient relationship.

**Why the Affair Recovery Workshop is the Essential Companion to this Book**

1. In-depth Guidance: While the book lays a solid foundation for understanding infidelity and the recovery process, the video program dives deeper into the critical topics, offering 2.5 hours of expert guidance from Jeffrey D. Murrah. The extended format allows for a more thorough exploration of the strategies and techniques needed to rebuild trust, improve communication, and foster intimacy.

2. Interactive Experience: The video program provides an engaging and interactive learning experience that complements the book. With visual aids, real-life examples, and guided exercises, you can actively apply the concepts and strategies to your own situation, enhancing your understanding and retention of the material.

3. Personalized Approach: The Affair Recovery Workshop recognizes that every couple's situation is unique. The video program offers a personalized approach, helping you identify and address your relationship's specific challenges and dynamics. This targeted guidance can accelerate healing and lead to more effective outcomes.

4. Convenient and Flexible: With 24/7 access to the self-paced video modules, a comprehensive 68-page workbook, and a bonus ebook, "How Can I Trust You Again?", you can work through the program at your own pace, from the privacy and comfort of your own home. This flexibility ensures you can fully engage with the content and implement the strategies on your own terms.

**Real Testimonials from Transformed Lives**

"The Affair Recovery Workshop was the turning point in our healing journey. Jeffrey's in-depth guidance and personalized approach helped us navigate the complex emotions and rebuild our marriage stronger than ever." - Sarah and Michael, married 9 years.

"The interactive experience of the video program, combined with the practical exercises in the workbook, allowed us to dive deeper into understanding and addressing the unique challenges in our relationship. It was a game-changer for us." - Lisa and David, married 14 years.

**Your Journey to a Stronger Marriage Starts Here**

Invest in your marriage and your future happiness with the Affair Recovery Workshop. As a special offer exclusively available to readers of this book, we're extending a 30% discount on the workshop to help you start your transformative journey. Don't wait - this offer won't last forever. Visit www.AffairRecoveryWorkshop.com and use the coupon code BOOK30 to claim your discount today.

Don't let infidelity define your marriage. Take the first step towards healing and renewal today, and give yourself the best opportunity to achieve the transformation you seek. With our 30-day unconditional guarantee, you have nothing to lose and everything to gain.

**What You'll Receive:**

- In-depth video modules (2.5 hours of expert guidance)

- 68-page comprehensive workbook

- Bonus ebook: "How Can I Trust You Again?"

- 24/7 access to the self-paced program

- 30-day unconditional guarantee

- Strictly confidential participation

By combining the insights from the book with the immersive experience of the Affair Recovery Workshop, you'll be equipped with the knowledge, tools, and support needed to overcome the devastation of infidelity and build a stronger, more resilient marriage.

Take action now and claim your 30% discount on the Affair Recovery Workshop. Visit www.AffairRecoveryWorkshop.com and use the coupon code BOOK30 to start your transformative journey today. Your satisfaction is 100% guaranteed.

Wishing you all the best on your path to healing and rediscovering the love and connection you deserve,

Jeffrey D. Murrah, LPC, LCDC

www.ingramcontent.com/pod-product-compliance
Lightning Source LLC
Chambersburg PA
CBHW052106150726
48002CB00006B/2238